God ... Send Me a Builder!

The Builder vs. The Borrower

Picture courtesy of Paul Ward's Photography, Raleigh, NC

Pastor Gregory W. Covington II

The Builder vs. The Borrower

Copyright © 2013 Gregory W. Covington II

www.GCovingtonBooks.com

All rights reserved. Published 2013
Printed in the United States of America
Library of Congress Control Number: 2013913317
ISBN 10:061585026X
ISBN-13:978-0615850269

DEDICATION

I want to dedicate this book to that perfect part of me; my wife. Thank you for the many years of love and support you've afforded me. You have unselfishly rescued me from a life of Borrowing and now I have become the Builder that God has called me to be. Although we've faced our challenges, you never gave up. When I tossed and turned at night from the stress of it all, it was your prayers that comforted me. It is with overwhelming joy that I can report; God gave me the best when He gave me you.

i

Also, to my wonderful kids, I love you all so very much. You make my life worth living. I'm looking forward to the next family get together at the house, and yes; no matter the weather, the grill is on!

Lastly, I dedicate this living manual to all of the Builders who have been called by the grace of God, for this very purpose. I charge you with the authority of the Father, to quickly fulfill your assignments. Strengthen each other in love and continue to hold each other in prayer. Be vigilant in guarding your anointing, for the enemy desires to sift you like wheat. In all things, give thanks and may the peace that passes all understanding guide your hearts.

ACKNOWLEDGMENTS

I'd like to acknowledge the prayers and support of my extended family: Bub, Melissa, Danny, Cindy, the Peppers, Mama Gloria, and Dad Cyril. Without your love and resurrecting support of me, I would still be undone. Likewise, I would also like to acknowledge a very special woman; Mrs. Corretta Allison, of the A List Inc. Thank you for seeing the potential in me and driving me from the backseat, to the driver's seat. Your tireless efforts are truly beginning to pay off, and I wish nothing but exceeding great things for your life.

I would also like to acknowledge my brothers in ministry: Apostle J.D. Stockton, Pastor Shannon Robinson, Pastor Donte' Jackson, Pastor Jameil Sanders, Pastor Brian Crawford, Minister Martin

Easley, Minister Alfred Wells, and all of my covenant brothers in arms. Keep spreading the word of truth. Special thanks to all the individuals who provided pictures for this writing. I appreciate your time, your temperance, and your talent. Dr. Christine Majette, thank you for always being a true friend and loving the real me. A very special thank you to Dr. Bernadette Elijah and Pastor Monique Walker Davenport.

Last, but certainly never least, I would like to acknowledge my good friend; my mentor, Dr. J.D. Carpenter. Not only have you been an inspiration, you have been the Graduate School instructor that has made a difference in my life. Thank you for your dedication to excellence.

FOREWORD

This tool for deliverance was placed in my hands and I rejoice with anticipation that you are having the opportunity to have it in yours. The scholarly and scriptural explanation of persons and situations that borrow and break us down, leaving us needing help, brings clarity. Our author paints a host of scenarios in an almost musically theatrical and intellectual way with his word brush. Technicolor flashbacks of realizations presented herewith, led to revelation and understanding in my own life, as it will in the lives of countless other individuals.

Spanning more than 30 years of ministry as a wife, mother, and spiritual leader, this book presented me with more of those ever so needed, self-diagnosing 'aha' moments. Many will have to acknowledge that with so many withdrawals from us, and few or no deposits, we've been harboring borrowers in our hearts, in our homes, and even in our churches. This revelation caused a light to shine and Acts 20:32 broke through from the pages.

" And now, brethren, I commend you to God, and to the word of his grace, which is able to build you up, and to give you an inheritance among all them which are sanctified"

These truths will dismiss from lives, what is no longer allowed; creating a place for the builders that will help us get to our promised inheritance. Those of us who have the privilege of being responsible for others, will take our calling and purpose to another realm; making the necessary covenant shift to become the loving, giving, responsible builder God requires of us.

While principles for the building of businesses, corporations, and organizations, are plentiful, here is your manual for becoming a builder of people created in the image of God. So, brace yourself, and allow God to use Gregory Covington II, who has become a builder through these pages, as your guide to bible-backed revelations answering many of the questions we face as Christain believers today. My only regret is not having this work when I was a Dean of a Bible College. This would have been on every students required booklist.

God...Send me a builder- begins as a request. To whom much is given much is required. God...Send me. Prayer answered.

~ Dr. Bernadette Elijah

INTRODUCTION

Since creation, women have been under attack. The enemy has launched campaign after campaign to deter you from your mission in hopes of causing a separation between you and God. Pastor Covington strategically explains why you have faced so much opposition. It seems as if for every step forward, you were pushed, pulled, or held two steps back.

The enemy has attacked your mind, your body; and now he's after your very soul because he knows that there is a perfect replica of God on the inside of every woman. He wants to shut down the 'machine'. If he can stop you before you deliver, then his mission will have been accomplished.

However, as you will discover; it's your time now. The enemy is terrified of what's growing within your spiritual womb. That's why you've been hated. Now, you can understand why you've been feeling the way you feel. You have grown sick and tired of all the bad decisions, and all the fruitless relationships for a reason. Surprise! You're pregnant. You've been experiencing some of the symptoms of your pregnancy. Don't worry; you're not in this thing alone.

There is a builder that's anointed and assigned just for you because, that which you have to birth out of your spirit, can only be secured by the builder. The borrower has taken your very last, and after you read, and re-read this powerfully transformative book, you too, will be screaming, "God…Send Me a Builder!"

God ... Send Me a Builder!

THE BUILDER VS. THE BORROWER

~ A Healing Manual for Women ~

PASTOR GREGORY W. COVINGTON II

God, Send Me a Builder

Photo of Lorenzo Wood by Jaboy Photography, Institute, WV

Photo courtesy of Paul Ward's Photography, Raleigh, NC

It is a known fact that the average woman is subjected to scenarios that would ordinarily cripple the average man. In fact, I had the pleasure of watching the latest superhero movie and I recall thinking that this guy has been beaten, abused, distrusted, and even rejected, but managed to overcome insurmountable odds. That's when the thought hit me; perhaps women could use some form of superman in their lives to make their load easier to bear. After all; I'm sure that the source of a lot of their struggles, has to do with relationships; both interpersonal, and how things become relative to them. But after much deliberation, I came to the conclusion; that would only suffice as an external covering, and that's just half the battle.

Historically, women have had to deal with molestation, spirits of rejection, feelings of inadequacies, torture, rape, violence, mental abuse, child bearing, menstrual issues/complications, self-identity crises, self-worth issues, brokenness, and heartaches. I could go on and on, but I would only be scratching the surface. Now on top of all those issues, many can add bad decision making, unproductive relationships, and plain old-fashioned 'no good men' tearing them apart from the inside out. Where does it end? With so much going on internally, you may ask yourself, 'how can I understand who am I, or whose am I'?

It's not a big secret that women are the weaker sex physically. In a society where the weak are preyed upon, women often suffer the brunt of the abuse, yet are expected to act like women. For all of your suffering, you are offered a fraction of what a man can earn, and if you play your cards right; perhaps a seat at the far end of the table. Struggle is nothing new to you; you have been prepared for that in your childhood, and that's assuming that your childhood innocence wasn't taken from you. While men have built statues to represent your beauty, they have also desecrated your earthly temples and stripped you of your dignity. Objectified; you now feel void of value because you've been told far too often that what you won't do, another woman will. With tears of regret, you've shamefully experienced that feeling of cheapening yourself just to hold on to something that you knew you should have never held to begin..

Let's not even go down the road of hurt and resentment. Each time your maternal heart reached out; rejection broke it. Every time you've sought asylum in the company of whom you deemed to be your peers, you were resented. People laughed at you because you didn't look like them, dress like they dressed, or acted as one of them. Ironically, some women have allowed the disapproving comments and stares of other women, to cause them to give up their virginity to someone not even worth their time. Confused; you waddle in self-loathe trying to hide the disdain behind layers of cover-up and mascara.

Some women psychologically hate to look at themselves in the mirror because it reflects the very thing they detest the most; themselves. They will outwardly continue to try and reconfigure themselves through cosmetics, surgeries, piercings, or whatever means they can afford, just to avoid seeing themselves as they originally were; it's too traumatizing for some. Perhaps, if it was only an occasional thing, you could manage it a bit better because the totality of your situations wouldn't hit you all at once, but we are talking about years of struggle and layers of unbridled inner rage. Some women have silently become angry at the system, angry at the source, and even angrier at themselves for allowing themselves to be taken advantage of, and for what? What did you receive for your surrender? Was it a simple fulfillment of lust from a partner who was never interested in anything more? Was it worth the emotional attachment, or spiritual detachment, which left you with a name you wish was never associated with your character?

I know what you're thinking. Not me right? I have it all together. Well, perhaps you do, but for those who can identify with some of the issues here, there is good news. The good news is that you're not alone despite how empty you feel; neither are you the first to go through this vicious cycle. In fact, would you believe me if I told you that some of the women in the bible felt the same way, or had some of the same issues? You will see that many of their real life stories are reflective of what you're dealing with today. Since there is nothing new under the sun, as much as your situation is new to you, it's not new to God.

If you've read along thus far, you should have noticed that I have strategically used the word "issues" when mentioning the plight of women. Problems are one thing, but an issue causes one to lose blood, or rather; life. I've learned in life that every problem has a solution, but recall the woman with the issue of blood as is written in Luke 8:43.

Luke 8:43,

"And a woman having an issue of blood twelve years, which had spent all her living upon physicians, neither could be healed of any…" (KJV).

There are two key points about this scenario you must understand. First, I want you to look closely at what she was losing. Next, I need you to understand the escalatory rate at which she was losing it.

She was losing blood, which is the quintessential carrier of life within the body. The body is so dependent upon blood being pure, that any contamination, coagulation (clotting), or disconnection from the oxygen needed to sustain it, can cause sudden death.

Picture of Tiffany Harris by Jaboy Photography, Institute, WV

Blood is one of the few internal components that actually touch every point within the body; from your lower extremities, to the crown of your head. I won't bore you with the biological study of blood and the fact that it is a connective tissue, but that should tell you something already. The fact remains that from her head to her toes, this woman was losing life.

A quick side note for you to remember is that the blood requires oxygen in order to work properly. When we inhale, oxygen is the least of the elements we take in at or near 20%. Nitrogen is dominant at roughly 78 %. Unfortunately, our lungs are not designed to use Nitrogen to survive, so we simply exhale it out. With this in mind you should understand that you were already conditioned by God, to survive on less. Don't waste any more time worrying about what you don't have, or how little you've been made to feel. Simply understand that you are sustained by less, and that in your less, you have life, and in your having life, you have the power to reproduce more.

The second thing that stands out about this woman with the issue of blood is that her condition became exacerbated from a simple problem, to an issue. I mentioned earlier that every problem had a solution, but as you can clearly see, this woman's problem escalated into an issue which caused her to lose life. If you can imagine a severity scale; the loss of things can be problematic but that's just one end of the scale. The losing of life would be at the other end of that scale; it's an issue. I know that you have gone through many emotional battles with many of them leaving scars of remembrance. Some of you may have recovered, in some sense, with the agony of knowing that you'd never be the same again. The grim reality is that many of you have had your problems heightened into issues, which have begun to draw life from you.

Some of you have wondered what happened to your visions and dreams; your aspirations are no longer a desire. You have started to settle for things that you were adamant against, and why? Why have you settled in the position of, 'this is just whom I am.' That's not who you are, but who you were made to be. Those traumatizing episodes you've experienced have become issues which have drained the blood, or the life, right out of your hopes and dreams. You're not weak, but you've become weakened. You're not financially irresponsible, but have difficulties maintaining your money. Because of the issues you have either dealt with, or are still facing, the life of your finances, your sanity, your emotions, and in extreme cases; your future, are being drained. While this may not apply to all women, all women should understand the difference between a problem and an issue because the Bible declares that the power of life and death is within the tongue. Don't call upon yourself an issue if it's just a problem. If it is a problem, then you can find a solution; so don't stress too much. If it is indeed an issue, then you have to understand the rest of what Luke noted in that verse. In short, he told you that no one could heal her even after she gave all she had.

How many times have you given your all to something or someone, only to have the same issue? You've tried remedy after remedy but you're still losing life; that's an issue. Can I make it clearer? Some of you have sown your tithes and offerings in church after church, but still the issue remains; you're losing life. In this woman's case, she gave all she possessed; everything she had, to doctors with the hope of being healed. You may not have the issue she suffered in the flesh, but struggling with your self-esteem is an issue. Promiscuity is an issue. Feeling unwanted, unloved, and uncared for, are all issues and going to "Dr. Johnny makes me feel good" has still not healed you from it. Some of you have tried "Dr. Illegal drugs" and still no relief.

An issue causes one to hemorrhage; always from the inside out. The abuse from your past has caused a hemorrhaging issue from your inside out. You don't even look the same as you used to; your smile is gone. I know that daddy shouldn't have left you alone, but he did. Because he did, you've had to endure some things that you weren't prepared to deal with, and now you're hemorrhaging from the inside out. You've tried to put a bandage on the affected area, but the hemorrhaging persisted. Now, we will deal with the source of the issue.

True healing begins at the source of the ailment; otherwise, we are just nursing a profusely open wound prone to an even greater infection. The body cannot heal that way; it always heals itself from the inside out. One of the greatest defenses of the human body, and the first source of protection, is unbroken skin. The only problem with skin, and I pray that you can see this in the spiritual as well, is that while it may be thick in some areas, it's thin in others. Certain areas of the skin are so thin that it becomes easy to tear; the perfect target of an invading enemy who enjoys attacking the weak points. Once invasion occurs, the enemy seeks to take over your control center.

The body is controlled by the great machine within your head, but sometimes it becomes rather noisy within our thought centers. We hear so many possible solutions that it's hard to hear the one that we should be listening to the most. Life screams at you, relationships pull on you, children depend on you, and the job only tolerates you, but where are you, if not all over the place? How can you hear that still small voice when it's being drowned out by your shameful past or the calamity of your shattering future?

Many may believe that time is a healer of all things, but in your reality, time is of the essence. Bills are due. Your children need provisions now. The rent is past due, and the weight of it all, now rests, squarely upon your shoulders. In your reality, you have had to become mother and father; nurturer and provider. Even in the home with your husband, and that's for those who have been fortunate enough to find their Mr. Right, you have had to take on extracurricular duties just to pick up the slack. As much as you have struggled throughout your wearisome day, you make it home in hopes to find rest, but are confronted with chaos and disruptions. In fact, you may have worked a full day only to come home and realize that the real work has just begun, and all you want to do is scream. Although this may be your reality, this is not the overall reality God has in store for you. It's okay to declare, 'I'm tired'; tired of the anguish; tired of feeling defeated.

Allow me to share this truth with you. You, yes cute little you, have been targeted by the enemy. For many years, and far too many church services, I've listened to, and have even preached about how the enemy is staunchly attacking the male seed. The truth of the matter is that there is a plan of attack over the lives of men, but that's the enemy's second wave of attack. His primary mission is to destroy women. If he can discredit your worth, confuse your mind, or change your identity, then he can find his way into destroying you from the inside out; remember hemorrhaging? Let me prove it to you now.

Genesis 1:1 (KJV) tells us that in the beginning, God created. His creation of life began with himself in mind. This is why man looks like

Him. He loves to see His image in us. In fact, He only responds to His image in us, and not to our imperfections. I'll elaborate more on that in just a bit. The only caveat that He intentionally omitted from man, was the ability to create life as He did. So, in His infinite wisdom, he placed that replicating power of creation, in the womb of a woman. Science is still trying to figure out God's afterthought, and this is coming from someone with a Bachelors of Science degree in Biology. Case in point; the double helix structure of DNA wasn't even discovered until 1952.

It was His plan for man to reproduce in His likeness.

Genesis 1:28,

"And God blessed them, and God said unto them, Be fruitful, and multiply, and replenish the earth, and subdue it: and have dominion over the fish of the sea, and over the fowl of the air, and over every living thing that moveth upon the earth." (KJV)

After being subdued by the enemy, we learn that in Genesis 3:16 (KJV); God greatly multiples Eve's sorrows and conception; stating that she will bear children through her sorrow. For their disobedience, mankind was forced out of the Garden of abundance, and into the land of desolation. The punishment associated with Adam was hard labor; his workload intensified. Not that this punishment wasn't stern enough for Adam, but if you recall, Adam was created to work. He was ordered by God, to name everything; that took work. Eve received a harsh punishment as well in that now, she would have to suffer agony through her reproduction of life.

Since Adam and Eve were created by God's own hand, the enemy could not destroy them; he could only convince them through an open ear. Right about now, would be a good time to give God praise because you too, were hand created by God. So, for as much as the enemy has tried to destroy you, he cannot. He can throw everything at you, but cannot break you. Even while Christ was being cruicified, the enemy thought that he was winning, but God wouldn't suffer the bones of Jesus to be broken. The enemy can try as he may, but God will not allow him to break your bones. Though the battle may intensify, you have unbreakable bones.

I am convinced that Satan's target wasn't Adam and his job; he wanted to destroy that perfect replica of God, within Eve. Even today, the enemy's main target is your God given, and God resembling, mechanism to reproduce. In short, he's still targeting the womb of women. It is his plan to throw you so far off course from your destiny that you will not be able to reproduce spiritually.

As a woman, you come under heavy attack because you carry a perfect part of God within you, and the enemy can't stand it. It's not even so much of the natural process of reproduction, but it's all about what you are capable of reproducing. Have you ever noticed how important this spiritual reproduction is to God? It's not by happenstance that His anger was kindled against Eve in Genesis 3:16, when He intensified her conception. God was angry at the fact that the enemy was able to manipulate something that He created perfect. He then demonstrated how He initially wanted it to be in John 3:16, which proves,

"For God so loved the world that He gave His ONLY begotten Son, that whosoever believeth in Him should not perish, but have everlasting life." (KJV)

God offers, as a sacrifice, his only offspring. Offsprings are the product of reproduction. Reproduction begins with a seed. Do you better understand the connection between the woman and the seed; the cyclic reproduction of life? This is why the enemy seeks to destroy you through confusion, feelings of worthlessness, and despair. He wants you barren so that spiritually, you will not be able to carry the offspring of his demise. Now, let's see his plan of attack.

In the natural sense, he attacks your mind from every angle possible in an attempt to cause you to surrender your spiritual rights to reproduction. Physically, he cannot take it from you by force, so his plan is still the same as with Eve; he wants your uncovered ear. How many times have you heard folks talking about you, laughing at you, or putting you down? The enemy is the master at confusing sound. Have you ever heard something that someone didn't really say, but you are certain that you'd heard it? The next thing you know, it looks like everyone is looking directly at you, as if you had two heads. Why not? At times, it certainly felt that way.

Now think of the number of times situations have forced you to recoil instead of launching out. When you should have been gaining traction in one area, you were losing place in another. No matter how high up the ladder you climbed, you still had so much further to go. Have you ever given any thought as to why you have historically made the same bad decisions, or dated the same caliber of men; ultimately making the same mistakes over and over again? No, it's not you; it's whom you've been shaped into.

Everything surrounding us, tends to bend us into conformity at times. No matter how much we try to think outside the box, the box only gets bigger and seemingly, more inescapable. Being natural receivers and incubators, you were fashioned to hold things internally. I have no problem confessing that women are internally stronger than men. Herein, lies the problem; and again think hemorrhaging. What happens when all of the hurt and pain of yesteryear, ages within you as you mature? As much as you desire it to be so, do you think for a moment that they disintegrate with maturity? On the contrary, they grow as you grow until they begin to form a life of their own. While with maturity your spiritual birthing hips take form, the immaturity from past circumstances, precedes the birth canal, causing you to become conceivers of hatred, malice, lust, and all other manners of evil. Since reproduction requires a seed and an egg, you can understand that your disposition, or issue, is not solely your fault; you simply received of its seed. Then; the machine began to do what it was designed by God to do, so the incubation process began.

Are you aware of the fact that there are people, and situations, designed simply to hate you? Yes, you have haters. No matter how much you try to love, and do right by everybody, you still have haters. Let's first, deal with how situations hate you.

Romans 8: 36-39

"As it is written, For thy sake we are killed all the day long; we are accounted as sheep for the slaughter. Nay, in all these things we are more than conquerors through him that loved us. For I am persuaded, that neither death, nor life, nor angels, nor principalities, nor powers, nor things present, nor things to come, Nor height, nor depth, nor any other creature, shall be able to separate us from the love of God, which is in Christ Jesus our Lord." (KJV)

Romans 14:11

"For it is written, As I live, saith the Lord, every knee shall bow to me, and every tongue shall confess to God." (KJV)

I'm certain that if you've ever attended a Sunday school class here or there, you have heard these scriptures before. Have you ever truly taken notice that the Apostle Paul is convinced that nothing will separate him from the love of God, but he includes, not just people, but what we consider situations? He purposed that both life (situation) and death (situation), nor *things* present (situation) or *things* to come (future situations), will separate him from God. How could he make mention of 'situations' or 'things', as if they were 'individuals' set to attack him? Here's where Romans 14:11 comes into play. The Lord himself, has declared that every knee shall bow and every tongue will confess unto him. Paul understood that since God is the creator of all things, then those *things* that opposed him, have to have been created. Understanding their creation, Paul deduced that instead of seeing his negative circumstances as something as broad as what he was caught up in (situation), he realized that it was simply something that he held hands and walked with in agreement. If it can move with you, talk with you, deceive you, and walk with you, then it has a tongue and a knee, and it's only at the name of Jesus that its knee shall bow. Yes, here's a spiritual truth; no, you're not caught up in poverty; you just walk hand in hand, agreeing with that spirit. I know you thought that you've struggled with depression, but the truth of the matter is that you weren't a victim of it; you walked hand in hand with it. The remedy is not deep at all; simply let go of its hand. If you don't want to be alone anymore, let go of the hand of loneliness. If you desire to healed; no need to run from one conference to another, just let go of the hand of brokenness and grab a hold to the hand of your healer.

Amos 3:3

God, Send Me a Builder

"*Can two walk together, except they be agreed?*"
(KJV)

Now, let's take a look as to why people hate you. You're hated for who you are, what you have, and where you're headed. Hatred has a way of embedding itself within the hearts and minds of some of our closest family members and friends. No matter how hard you try to fit in, you simply cannot get in. For whatever reason, to some, you are not pretty enough, smart enough, strong enough, and you don't earn enough to be included as 'one of'. All of a sudden you find yourself with your head hung low because you've accepted, or received, the depiction of others, as your own. You have willingly received their seed of hatred, and incubated it with the egg of your consciousness.

Oftentimes, it becomes difficult to determine those who are genuinely there for you, and those who hate you. As far enough on the spectrum as this should be, the lines become blurred at times;

especially when it comes from people we hold dear, like family. Camouflage was invented to disguise and deceive the opposing team from the very present danger they were facing. It is still in high usage today; not just on the battlefields of war, but on the battlefields of our hearts. Oddly enough, I wish that I could welcome you as the first partaker of this phenomenon, but the hatred of women; especially women with a true purpose, has been recorded from Genesis.

Genesis 29:31

"And when the Lord saw that Leah was hated, He opened up her womb: but Rachel was left barren." (KJV)

Here is a perfect example of many women today. The reason why you are bombarded so heavily is because of what you have to birth out of yourself. As you can see in this scripture, along with a few other women of importance which I will get to later;

Leah was hated. Just as I demonstrated the escalation of a problem to an issue, there is a significant difference between dislike and hatred. If dislike was a dime, then hatred would be a dollar.

Leah is much like many women today. She had her own flare and her own look, but was not accepted by any. Even her own sister Rachel, mocked her. Over time, I believe that Leah began to receive all of the criticisms, all of the accusations, and all of the contempt from people everywhere because seemingly; she did not fit in. Simply put; Leah was not wanted. How many times have you, yourself, felt unwanted or unloved? Nothing you did seemed good enough, and nothing you desired came quick enough. Do you remember the feeling of being lied on, mentally abused, or ridiculed just because? How many times were you called ugly, ignorant, and even worse names because you didn't stand out, or even put out? Leah found herself on the receiving end of hatred just because she didn't look like everyone else, and around this point in her life, it began to affect her mentally because she accepted it.

All of a sudden, her father; just like the Good Father above, gave her a companion in the form of Jacob, who was anointed from his mother's womb. I need to emphasize the point that he was anointed from his mother's womb, to demonstrate yet again, the importance of why the enemy desires to make you barren in spirit – he's afraid of what you have been ordained to birth.

Allow me to digress for a moment. The anointing on Jacob's life included his ability to build. When a man begins to walk upright before God, a part of his anointing has to do with some level of building; not just in the natural sense, but in the spiritual sense. We are not anointed of ourselves; that would profit us nothing. If you were anointed just for yourself, then you would not be productive in the Kingdom of God because the anointing supersedes us. Under the anointing of our lives, we draw dying men and women to God; thus, building the Kingdom of Heaven. Many of us are even anointed to build each other; this is the main premise of this manuscript, but when we don't understand the anointing on our lives, we become borrowers.

The borrower is one who consistently takes without ever having the ability to repay. He borrows the little you already exist on; leaving you worse off than when he found you. Although the borrower's intentions are good, good intentions are never good enough, neither are they Godly enough. The borrower is often camouflaged with good looks, pretty eyes, a muscular physique, and other unimportant attributes that women swoon over. In today's language, he may have the swag with the jag to match, but he's still a borrower. He can head Fortune 500 companies with his many advanced degrees, but without God in his life, he's just an educated borrower. Not even church can hide him. If he doesn't fully commit himself unto God; he can lead praise and worship, be the musical director, even the preacher himself, but he's still just a church going borrower.

The anointing is transformational, when we understand who we are. It is the catalyst that transforms mere men, into builders. Just what's so important about being a builder? The builder is skilled in construction. He can take something broken and dilapidated, and reconstruct it into something beautiful. In the palm of his hands lies the strength to re-erect what has been torn down. He is equipped; or rather anointed, to cover, to mend, heal, rejoin, reinvigorate, educate, and make whole everything he comes into contact with. Not only is it his passion, but because of the anointing on his life, it is his call. Just as messy and confusing, a construction site may look in the beginning; when a woman has been hurt by the hands of the borrower, only the hands of the builder can heal and make her whole. You can try all the therapy you want, all the clubs and alcohol you can drink, and all the care and comfort you think you can receive from other women who have been in your position; it will not work. But once you have experienced the hands of a builder reconstructing and replenishing what the borrower took from you, you will then be made complete. Unfortunately for the anointed Jacob, during that period of his life, his focus was skewed; causing him to lose sight of whom he was.

While there are contrasting differences between the borrower and the builder, the worse thing imaginable is an anointed builder operating as the borrower. It wasn't enough for the anointed Jacob, whom God said He loved before even exiting his mother's womb, not to operate as the builder for Leah, but he consistently became her borrower. Leah was heartbroken, ridiculed, and rejected by many, so the last person she would expect to reject her, would be her own husband. Can you imagine, or rather; have you been to the point where you've struggled with the tiny bit of dignity you had left, but all of a sudden the relationship that you thought would restore you took that last ounce from you? You just knew for sure that you had found the one, but in the end, you were left barely having a roof over your head.

The Builder vs. The Borrower

Your relationships have been uneventful at best, and why? Didn't you give yourself to him? Didn't you trust him with your heart and home? Didn't you find a way to finance his habits, wants, and desires; often putting yours on the back burner, and in the end, weren't you the one left further in debt? I am sorry to report that you fell in love, or lust, with the borrower. As blissful as it may have been in the beginning, the relationship was doomed to fail. As wonderful of a lover he may have been, his loving was only another form of borrowing. The worst thing you can do now is to continue pining for the borrower to return anything to you. Why have you waited for his phone call, only to suffer the more? You have cried tears after tear declaring you've had enough but have so easily allowed yet another borrower into your heart. Leah did the same thing, but what made her case especially heinous, is the fact that she was married to her borrower. It wasn't so easy for her to walk away, nor did she want to. All Leah desired was the affection of her husband, but was only offered the rejection of her borrower.

Time after time, she gave herself to him in hopes of moving beyond her hated past. What I love most about this moment in Leah's life, is the fact that the scriptures declare that the Lord saw her when she was hated. I know that there are folks who despise the very thought of you, but you have to remain humble. Now is not the time to seek retribution, fly off the handle, or lose your sanity because the Lord is now watching. He is looking at you in enjoyment because everything that the enemy has thrown at you may have weakened you, but it could not destroy you. Hatred tried its best to subdue you, but you're still here. It tried to bring false allegations against you, but you still prevailed. At its best, it attempted to discredit your value by degrading you, and although you still bear the scars of agony, it could not destroy you. Now the Lord sees right where you are and the scripture demonstrates that He is now responding.

How is the Lord responding to you? The bible says that He is opening up your womb. Not quite the response you had in mind? Perhaps you wanted him to crush your haters, or at least cause them to feel as they have made you feel. Sorry, none of the above. He responds in a grander sense; He is opening your womb. You might as well get yourself prepared; you are about to become spiritually pregnant. Why? I bet the last thing you would want in this scenario is to bring an offspring into it.

Isaiah 55:8 (KJV)

"For my thoughts are not your thoughts, neither are your ways my ways, saith the Lord." (KJV)

When God has His eyes on you, you have to learn to expect the unexpected. His thoughts are higher than ours, and all that He does, is in fulfillment of His will. Sure, you've been wounded and maybe even left almost unrepairable, but I can assure you that since His eyes are on you, you have just received His undivided attention, and He is mending your situation in accordance to His perfect will.

The fact that he opens Leah womb when He sees that she is hated, tells me that at one point, she could have very well been barren. Just like Leah, I bet if you truly take note of your haters, you will see that the majority of them are other women. In her being hated; especially by her borrower husband, she gives herself to him and bears his first child Reuben. In her mind, she was expecting that when Jacob's seed met her need, then Jacob would be one with her; he would desire her. To her dismay, she was rejected and still hated by her borrower. He simply borrowed just a little more of the infinitesimal dignity she had left. It took Leah pulling together quite an amount of fortitude to knowingly give herself to this same man that didn't want her; only to have the last of her fortitude borrowed. The second time, she gathered as much resilience as she had left, and gave herself to him again. She conceived Simeon, but again, she was rejected as the borrower took the last of her resilience.

Imagine, for a moment, the injustice Leah felt knowing that the person who was supposed to be the closest to her, was in fact, the furthest from her. Can you imagine, better yet; how many times have you found yourself attached to the very anchor that was sinking your ship, while you casually allowed it to happen? Even if your borrower wasn't a man, it came in another form. Your borrower could have been your very past which borrowers the success you were destined for in your future. It steals from you; robs you of your identity and leaves you barren and unfruitful. If you have found yourself in the borrowed position at some point in your life, there's still hope because Leah witnessed a game changer. Again, Leah gave herself to her attached borrower expecting a different result.

Now, we've been told a time or two, that the definition of a fool is doing the same thing repetitively; expecting a different result. As much as we hate to admit it, we've all played the fool at some point in our lives. But Leah discovered something amazing this time around. Although she was rejected once again, she opted to focus more on what she had produced in this third child name Levi. Little did she know, or Jacob for that matter, that Levi would grow up and become the Father of the Levitical priesthood. Biblical history dictates that the Levitical priesthood was in essence, the priests who would usher in worship. Today, they would be called your worship leaders. If only Leah and the anointed borrower Jacob, knew what they had just produced. Sadly, the cycle continued.

Once again Leah decided that after everything she had been through; the hatred, the humiliation, the tears, the rejection; all of it, she was going to try one more time to win his affection. Have you ever gotten to the point where you've made up in your mind, that if it happens again, you were finished? You have tried all that you knew to do and were still unable to make ends meet. After all the times you loaned money to family and friends, who continued to take the little you had and never repay it back; you had finally reached your breaking point. You have gone out of your way to help people, feed folks who still don't like you, take from your own home to ensure better for someone else; only to still be laughed at, and talked about. Finally, you've had enough and have declared that this is the very last time. We've all been there. Some of us are at our breaking points right now and it doesn't feel good at all. You feel taken advantage of, prostituted, used, victimized, and punished without cause; yet, you humbly support, and continually provide. Well, Leah (you), there's still hope.

One more time, Leah gave of herself to her husband and again, like clockwork, she was rejected. This is where some women become judgmental of others. I can hear the voices of women today crying, 'No way, I would have taken all that.' Did I not mention earlier, that at some point, WE ALL have played the fool? It's so much easier to see the deterioration of others, but we cannot see it within our own affairs. The view is always different from the inside out; but Leah finally discovered what she was doing wrong. It's important to note that she did not change how she felt about herself inwardly. Sometimes, you can experience things in your life so frequently, that it becomes all you know to be true; it's now your disposition. The truth of the matter is that Jacob, the borrower, was never into her; he didn't desire her. Jacob wanted Rachel, her sister. No matter how many times Leah could have attempted to win over her borrower, she would have never prevailed. This is why she decided after conceiving this last child named Judah, she would then focus on God and not the borrower.

Indeed, after being rejected once again, she shifted her focus, but while she was yet conceiving Judah, she was still hated and rejected. Just so that you are aware, while you are carrying your Judah within your own womb, you will still be hated. If Leah was here today, she would simply tell you to shift your focus, shift your mind, shift your thoughts, shift your outlook; for the life of your seed, you have to shift.

Just so that we all better understand; Judah means praise, and if I can for just a moment, share with you the fact that the reason why you have been through the rapes and the beatings, the rejections and everything else that was meant to destroy your moment, is because of what you are carrying in your spiritual womb. Remember, the enemy is out to abort your labor because in your womb, grows a praise so great, that at the very sound of it, his kingdom crashes.

Jacob, the borrower, rejected Leah while she was pregnant with praise. Likewise, the reason why you are rejected is because there is a praise growing on the inside of you, that the enemy cannot stand. This is a great example as to why you, as a hated woman, cannot go to all the clubs and parties, because where you go, your Judah is traveling. Unfortunately, you can't eat and drink certain things while you're hated, because what you drink; Judah has to digest.

You already know that staying overnight with borrower after borrower is out of the question, because where you lodge; Judah sleeps. The reason why you wake up early mornings is because Judah is stretching out in your spiritual womb; and none of this ever happened until God saw that you were hated. Now imagine that! Because you are hated, talked about, lied on, held back, and taken advantage of, God is allowing you to give birth to your greatest weapons of self-defense; praise and worship.

Unfortunately, in the natural, Leah was still unaccepted, and no matter what some women do in their lifetime, they will suffer the same fate. Is acceptance by peers a priority in life especially when there's a builder willing to accept you just as you are? In her rejection, she not only became everything that Jacob, the borrower, needed, but everything she needed for her own salvation was birthed from her own womb. Some of you may be thinking to yourselves, 'well, that was so long ago; time has changed.' I submit to you this; not only did praise and worship cover her back then, but from Genesis until Revelation; the only way you could reach God, was through Leah's offsprings; praise and worship. From that generation until today; in order to reach heaven's gate, you have to have a relationship filled with praise and worship. Now, can you see how God's perfect plan for Leah's life worked in all of our favor? Here's another chance to give God a praise. Imagine just for a second, the product of your labor.

I cannot take anything from Jacob's anointing at all. Yes, he was anointed, but with Leah, he was only a borrower. He was Leah's borrower, but Rachel's builder. Sounds like quite a conundrum since he was married to both women. In other words, your borrower is someone else's builder. Rachel discovered that it is best to keep silent and wait for your builder to come. In her haste, she thought she was mocking her sister, but while God's perfect will was being completed over Leah's and Jacob life, she wasn't mocking Leah, she was mocking God; for that, he closed up her womb. God made her barren.

God, Send Me a Builder

While God wants to give you your heart's desire, He has to prepare you for it by giving you everything you need first. He will not afford your desires mocking the fulfillment of your needs; so he closed up the womb of Jacob's desire until he fulfilled all of his needs. I will reveal more on this story later.

What God has for you, is for you; so your builder is on his way, but he can't approach you when you are entangled with the borrower. The more the borrower takes from you, the more the builder has to restore. Stop wasting borrowed time, when now is the season to build. Don't be afraid to tell them that you're not interested; you're just waiting for your builder. Let them think that you are being conceded, when in actuality, you are simply counting down the moments until your builder arrives.

Life presents us with a series of decisions. We have to make decisions about how we present ourselves, what we should say, how we are to act, where we should go, and who we should keep company with. Decisions require thought. No matter how complex the situation may be, they require some logical progression culminating into a single conclusion. How simple right? Well, historically, the problem seems to stem from decisions we make, not from thought, but from emotions. Whether we want to admit it or not, we are all emotional beings; women and men as well. In fact, more often than not, we are moved when we feel like it, and the hardest thing for us to do at times, is to get our emotions under control. They often think for us, speak out of us, and even dictate to us, our positions. The danger in this is that our emotions are often shaped by outside influences. Logic is internal; we learn something, internalize it, and make decisions using the mechanisms of logic, but emotions, though also internal, are stimulated by outward extremes. When this happens, we really shouldn't trust our emotions, but not only do we trust them, we have a proclivity of allowing them to take the lead for us. When our emotions say get angry; we get angry. When it tells us to be sad, we can't help feeling sadness; never giving logic a fair chance; so when a logical solution would suffice, we can only offer an emotional resolution.

What happens when our emotions are shaped by violence? What occurs when we lead with our emotions of abuse? Of course, you will not play the victim again, which is why you are leading with a guarded emotion of secured safety; 'no one gets in here.' You have the right and all the reasons in the world to emotionally respond to the first person or situation, that reminds you of a devastating period in your life that you would rather put behind you for good. However; in all these instances, did you ever stop to think that you were leading with your emotions and not with sound logic? Suppose I saw you in a store and walked over to you to say, 'Good evening. I just wanted to tell you that I think you are a very attractive woman, but why do you feel you have to darken your beautiful eyes with so much make-up?' A good majority of women would immediately respond negatively because their guarded emotions trigger an irrational response. Although there may be truth in the fact that the make-up was too heavy, the truth is immediately rejected because emotions trump truth.

The builder and the borrower are advanced at breaking down emotional barriers; one positively, and the other for selfish gain. The paths that the two take are completely opposite; the builder builds the pathway to logical reasoning, while the borrower fights to keep you in a highly emotional state. He wants you to remain emotionally attached and dependent on him so that you don't become cognizant of his character. The borrower wants you to feel as if you've fallen in love with him, so that he can further his borrowing spree, but the builder wants to arrest your emotional state and help you to logically refocus on those attributes that really matter. The borrower majors in preferences, while the builder focuses on what's best for you.

Now, let's assume that the examples so far, have not represented the woman you are now. In fact, you've worked hard, made the right choices, and avoided negative influences. If this is you, then I applaud you. Your diligence has served you well and you should be commended. However, there you are one day, and out of the blue, something life-changing hits you right between the eyes. Your entire world is turned upside-down in a matter of moments, and now you find yourself, completely out of your element. Zlelponi, is a witness of such a life-altering event.

Through biblical research we discover that Zlelponi was a Judahite; thank God for the many Leah's out there. Being a Judahite meant that she either lived in Judah, or was from Judah; either way, she was accustomed to praise. She was trained, reared, and taught, to praise God from whom all blessings flow. I am convinced that she was on the right path, doing the right thing, and making the right connections for her life when she fell in love with a man named Manoah. Zlelponi may have had things together; much like yourself, but she was lacking just one thing; she was unable to bear children. Again, can you see the plan of the enemy to attack your ability to reproduce because he's afraid of the product of your labor?

Zlelponi and Manoah were married, but could not produce offsprings. No matter how hard they tried, no child was born into their union. Remember the struggle and turmoil in your own life when everything you've tried failed you? Some of us are well acquainted with the feeling of disappointment. During those days, having children was a sure sign of being blessed, and favored by God. In fact, Manoah's co-judge Ibzan, had sixty children and celebrated the marriage of each annually, but never invited Manoah and his barren wife. They were considered outcasts, in a sense, and because of such, they were hated.

Whether you know it or not, sometimes, people will hate you for something that isn't even your fault; you have no control over it, yet hated for it. You can not have a hand in it, but be hated for it all the same. Hatred knows no bounds. Zlelponi could have very well, tuned out the outside distractions and focused on her own house, but again; where do you turn when you are hated in your own home? Where is the peace?

Her husband; a good man, had to endure the ridicule of not being able to bear children. Perhaps, at some point, he accepted others dispositions as his position. Their insults became his crown, and he began to take it out on his wife. This is why it is imperative for married couples to cover each other with prayer. The enemy cannot successfully defeat a team because

Matthew 18:20 states:

"Where two or three are gathered together in my name, there am I in the midst of them." (KJV)

So, he devises a plan to attack one or the other; just as he did in the garden. The outside ridicule became too much for Manoah, and he began to ridicule his wife. All of a sudden, it's her fault that they could not produce children. From the outside looking in, it seemed as if the enemy's plan was working.

Zlelponi, from Judah (praise), was moved by her emotions. I can hear her in the spirit saying, 'you will not talk to me like that in my own home.' Now, the husband, who brought home the confusion from outside, is blaming the wife, and the wife; shifted into her emotional state, is blaming the husband. See how the enemy's plan to divide and conquer began to take shape? All it took was an open ear, and the plan was set in motion. Some of us can bear witness that all of a sudden; without warning, the peace in our own home was no longer there. We've all been there; when everything within our homes, within our relationships, or even in our workplaces, started and ended with some form of argument. The spirit of confusion will consume your mind, and before you know it, you will find yourself doing things you never imagined yourself doing. This is what happened to Zlelponi; and if you have found yourself nestled between a highly emotional state and confusion, then there's still hope.

Judges 13:3-5,

"And the angel of the Lord appeared unto the woman, and said unto her, Behold now, thou art barren, and bearest not: but thou shalt conceive, and bear a son. Now therefore beware, I pray thee, and drink not wine nor strong drink, and eat not any unclean thing: For, lo, thou shalt conceive, and bear a son; and no razor shall come on his head: for the child shall be a Nazarite unto God from the womb: and he shall begin to deliver Israel out of the hand of the Philistines." (KJV)

Expect the unexpected every time. For all of Zlelponi's agony, she found favor from the Lord, who opened up her womb; and when the Lord does it; don't expect the ordinary, look for the extraordinary.

There are three points I want you to see in this particular passage: the angel of the Lord confirmed that she was barren, but will conceive a son. Next; to be careful of what she consumes while she's pregnant, whether naturally or spiritually, and finally, that her son will begin to deliver Israel from the Philistines. The devil is busy, and in this case, he had his hands full. This is why he tried so hard to usher in the spirit of confusion. He wanted to disrupt the peace and unity within her home in order to cancel the assignment on her life; but his plan was beginning to crumble.

Here again, we have barrenness; the inability to reproduce, yet; God overturns this condition. It doesn't matter if we consent or not; God's will, shall always be done in our lives; that much, we cannot control. We can willingly choose to receive it, or be crushed by it; either way, He's God. We cannot go around him, and when we make up our minds to surrender all to him, He secures us under His wings. His vision for our lives always includes provision, but here is the miracle of God's provision; it's always in abundance. The abundance of His provision in

Zlelponi's life didn't just cover her, but generations as well. Remember Leah's babies?

The second point is in regards to consumption. Don't just think of consumption in the natural; although there are some things we should avoid, but in the spirit as well. You've heard the expression that everything is not for everyone; well it's true. We cannot spiritually consume all manners of evil without repercussions. In the natural, if you drink too much, you will find yourself drunk. We should live by the laws of temperance; not compulsion.

Toy companies make a fortune each year because children are compulsive; they want everything they see. In their innocent minds, it doesn't matter how much it costs, or how hard their parents have to work to get it; they want it, and they want it now. We can expect that from children, but as adults, our childish ways should be behind us. Impulsiveness breeds extensive consumption. We have a tendency to over-indulge in certain things, especially when we deem it as a pleasure. It's not enough, in our minds, to taste of it in moderation. We become drunk with the power of our impulsive overabundance. Truthfully speaking, many things we have are superfluous, but we desire them anyway.

The last point was that her son would begin to deliver Israel. Her son; the offspring that she could not have until the Lord intervened, would be anointed to begin to deliver all of Israel from the Philistines; these were giants. If you haven't figured out the son yet; it is Samson. Like Leah, it was already pre-arranged by God, that Zlelponi would give birth to her own deliverance. Bet you didn't know that you have been carrying your own deliverance in your womb all this time. You tried running from church to church for an answer that has been shut up in your own womb.

Here comes the anointed Samson. I am more than certain that if I were to ask ten women what they know about Samson, I would hear almost the same story. Anyone who has been to Sunday school twice knows the story of Samson; at least they think they do. I'm sorry; but I thought I mentioned to always expect the unexpected. You, of all people, should know that everything is not always what it appears. How many times have you been misjudged? People thought they had you all figured out, but because of the anointing on your life, and in your womb, God has concealed unto Himself, some glory on the inside of you, that can bring a nation to its knees.

Samson could be classified as a borrower, because he spent a good portion of his life borrowing from women, but he is also a builder. I'll prove it you in just a bit. You have to ask yourself this question, "If Samson was such a 'bad guy' then why would God open up his mother's barren womb, and anoint him to be a deliverer? Why would God seemingly waste his time? Don't worry; He wouldn't then and He doesn't now.

The story of Samson deserves a closer look. Much like us, Samson did foolish things. He was in fact, immature in some areas, and impulsiveness was his constant companion. He made mistakes and only had access to things because of who his father was. In his impulsiveness, he could ask his father for things, and his father would give it to him. Sounds like some of us. We have found ourselves being wayward at some point in our lives, but always had the ability to ask our Heavenly Father for something, and He would provide. No matter how much we messed things up, our Father loved us more than our mistakes. This is what I mean by God responding to His image in us, and not to our character flaws. One thing that you cannot deny about Samson is that he was anointed from his mother's womb. He may have been childish in some areas, but he was anointed. He didn't always do the right thing, yet; he was still anointed.

Let me just add the fact that many of us, are just like Samson. We are childlike in many ways, but we are anointed leaders. Samson's greatest problem was that he either didn't know the extent of his anointing, or didn't comprehend it; and that's right where many of us find ourselves today. We don't fully understand the anointing on our lives. Some of us haven't even begun to scratch the surface of who we are yet. We are up one day, and down for a few more. Sometimes, we can feel the presence of God, and other times, we feel abandoned by him. Just like Jacob, we find ourselves wanting those things that we desire (Rachel), but rejecting the things we need (Leah). But in all of these things, we cannot discredit the anointing of God on our lives. It is imperative that you understand, the anointing is never crowned on the head of perfection. In other words, God doesn't seek out perfect people; He anoints willing vessels. Stop holding your leaders infallible as if they are incapable of error. We are all humans; and while we breathe air, we are subject to temptation.

James 1:2,

"My brethren, count it all joy when ye fall into divers temptations..." (KJV)

This is not God's permission for us to habitually sin, but He wants us to know that nothing could fall unless it was first standing, and when you really think about it, that's the main reason why we fall in the first place. Let's face it, sometimes we simply don't feel God and we panic, so we slip and fall, but if and when you do; be certain to fall on the side of His grace, and get back up again.

Just like Samson, who fell time after time, you have the ability to shake yourself and watch the anointing overtake you. Don't worry about the ones who don't support you or the ones who judge you because of your character flaws. Samson proved that at any given time; whether he was up or upside down, he was anointed by God and nothing could change that.   You have an anointing on your life that is transformative.   Close your ears to idle talk, and become vigilant in your praise and worship.   Above all; guard the anointing that covers you.

Samson had the anointing of strength. Unlike herald superheroes, he was indeed a fallible man endowed with the strength of God. Let's look at this for just a moment. I had to ask myself, 'of all the attributes God could have anointed Samson with, why strength?' Solomon's anointing was wisdom, Paul's anointing was Apostolic, but why would God allow Samson to have superhuman strength? The reason is simple in nature. Samson's anointing of strength had to do with his purpose of fighting the Philistines; he had to fight giants. Here is yet another resemblance of many of us today. How many of us, have had to take down some giants? Did you know that a generational curse is a giant, and destroying that giant requires strength that you could not muster of your own accord? How many of us have been the first in our families, to graduate high school; go to college, own a home, or even pastor a ministry? Congratulations Samson, you've successfully destroyed some giants in your life; mission accomplished! Whether you know it or not, there were some strongholds over your life, over your job, and over your children, that only the anointing of strength could have taken down. I bet you thought you were struggling while breaking through the spirit of rejection. Many of you found yourselves physically drained after fighting through some hard fought victories, but you should have been because the anointing of strength was in action while you were fighting. The enemy thought he could gang up on you with giants of health related illnesses, family crisis, job layoffs, and even divorce, but the strength of God, brought you through your battles. I told you earlier that your bones won't be broken. You may bear some scars, but giants have been destroyed; mission accomplished.

The builder is well equipped to take down giants, in fact; they live for it. They study the art of slaying giants so that their relationships can be made whole. Their strength is unparalleled to mere humans and their selfless acts of protection; placing themselves in harm's way, secures the safety and sanctity of their environments. While they are mere flesh and blood, they may occasionally fall short, but they have the wherewithal to shake themselves so that the anointing would once again overtake them. They live to serve and serve to live.

The borrower turns into the beggar in the presence of giants. They retreat; turn around or quit when the going gets tough. Fearful of giants; instead of fighting, they are busy begging the giants to spare their lives. In the 15th chapter of Judges, the giants have cornered these borrowers in Judah. How can I know that these men of Judah at the time were borrowers? How easy was it for the giants to persuade them to turn on Samson, even after admitting that they did all they could to take Samson out and nothing worked? The real question here is how easy was it for the enemy to meet them in Judah? Recall that Judah means Praise. Since we are not selfishly anointed, Samson's anointing covered them as well, but somehow the enemy was able to persuade them in their praise; ok borrower. When they should have been covering the builder whose anointing covered them, they turned on him.

Here's another praise point. Have you ever been in a situation where your family or friends, have turned on you? When they should have been praying for your strength, they were plotting your demise. Perhaps, it was even in your church. Nobody but God knows how hard you've worked and how much you've sacrificed to lead praise and worship, but whenever you open your mouth, people questioned why you had to lead the songs, teach Sunday school, or collect the offering? When they should be celebrating you, they hate on you. But the good news is that they are proving you to be a builder; inundated with the anointing of strength.

Women, these Samson's; these anointed builders, are currently slaying giants to get to you and they cannot stop until the mission is complete. It may seem as if it is taking them so long to reach you, but that's only because there are so many giants that they have to destroy. The world grows wickeder and wiser with each generation. That means that these giants of today now have Facebook profiles, Twitter accounts, and all sorts of access to various social media networking. These giants now have internet access with easy capabilities of luring young children into pornography; stealing your identity, or arranging weapons of mass destruction. They have become sophisticated in the language of rebellion and have lured others to follow. Builders have been dispatched to track down and destroy these modern day giants; but have often been overlooked. Their deeds may go unnoticed, but they are still fighting. They may never have their own day of recognition on the calendar, but they never take a day off of the battlefield.

Samson's countrymen joined together to bind him, and deliver him to the enemy. What appeared to be his certain demise, became a valuable lesson for today.

Judges 15:14-15

"And when he came unto Lehi, the Philistines shouted against him: and the Spirit of the Lord came mightily upon him, and the cords that were upon his arms

became as flax that was burnt with fire, and his bands loosed from off his hands. And he found a new jawbone of an ass, and put forth his hand and took it, and slew a thousand men therewith." (KJV)

Samson became an educator of the anointing of God on that day. His lesson: never let the enemy forget how anointed you are. When it seems like the haters on your job, have gotten the best of you; shake yourself and declare, 'I AM ANOINTED FOR THIS'. Though many rise against you; sometimes, you'll have to shake yourself to remind yourself that you are still anointed. I know you may have slipped along the way, but the anointing on your life is keeping other people alive. Even during those days when you just don't feel like it, you are still anointed, and the anointing on you, keeps others alive.

Have you ever heard someone completely intoxicated begin singing a worship song unto God? Before you can blink twice, the alcohol dries up because the eyes begin to tear up as the anointing starts to fill the atmosphere. How is that possible? The bible declared that the gifts of God are without repentance, and the anointing is a gift; so in times of trouble, shake yourself and watch the anointing make the difference.

The bible laid the foundation of truth and declared that greater is He within you, than he that is within the world. You have to stand ready to draw upon the anointing in your life. A relationship with a man may be good, but it's the relationship with God that maintains the anointing over your life, over your children, and over your home. You are so anointed that even your enemies are covered by you. Now, imagine your anointed self, walking hand in hand with your builder. The bible states that one could chase a thousand but two could put ten thousand to flight. Didn't I mention that this was only the beginning for Samson?

While most believers think that his death was the end of him, God said in the beginning that Samson would just begin to deliver Israel, therefore; contrary to popular belief, his death was only the end of the chapter; not the end of Samson's story. Just like a lot of us, how many times were we told that we were finished? Our enemies have declared that it was all over for us, but little do they know that they've only witnessed the end of that particular chapter; our story isn't over yet. I'll explain more on that in just a few.

It's time for some of the trials that have been ongoing in your life, to cease. As destructive as storms may be, they only last for seconds; not centuries. The borrower can only perpetuate the suffering, but the builder has the power in their tongue to simply declare, 'no more.' The builder Joshua, decreed with a loud voice,

'...sun, stand thou still upon Gibeon; and thou, Moon in the valley of Ajalon' (Joshua 10:12).

You need a builder that has such a relationship with God that he can call those things in your life that have been troubling you year after year, to cease. He stands flat-footed in the face of the enemy and can cause the sun to stand still; and the sun must obey his command. The God in him can even control the season you walk in. Whereas you thought that you were past your prime, or missed your season, Naomi; the builder can reverse the time, and place you in the season of your greatest blessing. You may feel old in age, but the restorative anointing of the builder will cause you to nurse your greatest blessing on your lap. You can just ask Ruth who would tell you that no matter what; stay connected. Some things may die off along your journey, but stay connected.

Who is this builder that I keep referring to? What is his name? What does he look like? This builder comes in many forms. He's found in every nationality, every culture, every race, and every ethnicity. The builder can be found either in the halls of universities, or riding the bus home from work. How do you spot this builder? He's usually the one who has obtained favor from the Lord. He's a man of few words, but filled with praise. The God center of this builder resonates so heavily through him, that people are blessed just to be in his presence. His humility guides him. His God preserves him.

Picture of Isaiah Pauley taken by Sebrina Grose, Clay, WV

He is a warrior unlike any other; a strong man ready to defend your honor, restore your name, and protect your heart. What does he look like? He's hard to describe visually because his looks can be misleading. You may think he should look one way, but chances are, you've passed him by. You've become so entrenched with looks that you've walked by the builder on your way into the arms of the destructive borrower.

In the case of Samson, the Nazarite, his hair was nearly dragging the floor. When the angel of the Lord spoke to his mother, he instructed her not to let a razor touch his head. This builder could be in disguise like Jacob, who covered himself in goat hair, to receive the inheritance of his father's blessing. You're probably thinking about this scenario and wondering how was this fair; well it wasn't because there's nothing fair about the builder. I told you he found favor with God. Who are we to judge what's right and wrong when God himself, not only told his mother that he would turn tradition on its head by having the elder to serve the younger, but then went on to declare, 'Jacob I loved. Esau, I hated.'

The builder comes in all shapes and sizes too. I know you would prefer them to be slim to athletic build, but they may be a little on the heavy side because, like the prophet Elijah, God requires them to eat the whole roll so that His words would be in their mouth. I know that here in the United States, we have all kinds of health initiatives, but your builder could very well have an appetite addiction like Elisha, who couldn't help wanting a double portion. He may not carry the scent you desire because like Jonah; he may have found deliverance from the belly of a great situation that swallowed him whole. You could have walked passed him on the streets thinking he was some wild man without a home like John, who had to prepare the way for the Christ. Stop eye discerning the moment of your builder. If we could have it the way we want it, then why would we need God at all? If anything, pray for the strength of the builder because the enemy desires his head on a platter.

Notice how John the Baptist, always pointed to someone greater than himself? The builder will always point you in a direction other than himself because he knows that without God, he does not exist. He could even be small in stature; boyish in many ways, but he's out there tending to the sheep in the field – that means he's already a pastor at heart. Even his own family can overlook him like David, but in the eyes of God; he's a king.

King David, who was hand-picked as a king by God before being crowned a king by man, proved repeatedly that he was a builder. In the face of clear and present danger, this BOY would pick up the slack for full grown adult borrowers. Watch how the borrowers try to deduce him in stature. They will even try to adorn him in their armor, but it won't fit because the real battle is between the builder and the giants. I just told you that there was nothing fair about the builder; well, even the fight is favor-fixed. Just because the giants think that they have the advantage over the bare-knuckled, unarmed builder, they try to taunt him and downplay his strength. In their minds, he's no threat; no match for their superiority, but with a single stone and a slingshot; giants do fall!

Sometimes, the builder may not understand their moment, so they may be on the run, but even though they are, the anointing of the builder, still draws men unto them.

1 Samuel 22:1-2,

"David therefore departed thence, and escaped to the cave Adullam: and when his brethren and all his father's house heard it, they went down thither to him. And every one that was in distress, and every one that was in debt, and every one that was discontented, gathered themselves unto him; and he became a captain over them: and there were with him about four hundred men." (KJV)

What manner of man is this builder who can open his mouth and arrest borrowers; converting them into builders? He takes no credit for himself, but gives God all of the glory. And just in case you are wondering how all of this is connected, this particular builder, David, had a grandfather builder named Obed, who was the son of Boaz and Ruth of whom I mentioned was nursed on the lap of Naomi even after her prime. If Naomi was here today, she would tell you that it's never too late. God can do what man can only marvel at!

But builders aren't perfect; they are humbled clay worth perfecting. David proved this point when he borrowed Bathsheba. This is why it is ever so important for the builder to be in the right place of mind, body, and spirit. His eyes should never see what his God center could never digest. David laid his eyes on Bathsheba who was simply doing her normal, everyday routine. Instantly, the foundation of his relationship was shaken; not his natural relationship, but his relationship with God. Notice how I said it was shaken. What the enemy doesn't want us to understand is that our connection to God is unbreakable; even when we error, we're still connected.

Scientifically speaking; it requires a certain amount of strain or heat energy to break molecular bonds, but the bond between you and God, cannot be destroyed. How do I know this?

Psalms 139:1-14 declared,

"O Lord, thou hast searched me, and known me. Thou knowest my downsitting and mine uprising, thou understandest my thought afar off. Thou compassest my path and my lying down, and art acquainted with all my ways. For there is not a word in my tongue, but, lo, O Lord, thou knowest it altogether. Thou hast beset me behind and before, and laid thine hand upon me. Such knowledge is too wonderful for me; it is high, I cannot attain unto it. Whither shall I go from thy spirit? or whither shall I flee from thy presence? If I ascend up into heaven, thou art there: if I make my bed in hell, behold, thou art there. If I take the wings of the morning, and dwell in the uttermost parts of the

sea; Even there shall thy hand lead me, and thy right hand shall hold me. If I say, Surely the darkness shall cover me; even the night shall be light about me. Yea, the darkness hideth not from thee; but the night shineth as the day: the darkness and the light are both alike to thee. For thou hast possessed my reins: thou hast covered me in my mother's womb. I will praise thee; for I am fearfully and wonderfully made: marvellous are thy works; and that my soul knoweth right well..." (KJV)

David, the builder, found himself in a fallen borrower position. What's to be expected is that any man, builder or borrower, who takes his eyes off of God; sees everything ungodly. Once the builder David took his eyes off of God, he saw lust and desire. David sent for her; slept with her, then sent her home. Bathsheba was now pregnant by a borrower who was a king.

One thing about the builder in error; he knows when he's wrong. In an attempt to try and cover his tracks, the borrower David, tried to get her husband to sleep with her, and when that failed, he had him killed in battle. There are no limits the borrower will not sink to, to rob you of your sanctity. David married Bathsheba; but he was still a borrower. The bible declared that David greatly loved the child conceived with Bathsheba. Notice how easy it is for us to fall in love with our mess ups? How many times have we made the wrong decisions, but have loved the road it led us down? I never stated that borrowing wasn't fun; it's detrimental. David sinned, but fell in love with the sin he created. How comfortable is the borrower in his broken position? He tries his best to make his world make sense all around him; knowing that he is living a borrowed life. Selfishly, the borrower continued his ruse until one day, the prophet Nathan, reminded the King that he was found prostrate in the borrowing position.

Recall the connection I stated that the builder has with God. God has too much invested in him to allow him to stray too long. The builder has an assignment to keep and an appointed time to keep it in. God will not allow a builder turned borrower, to abort his mission. The Bible declares that He chastens those that he loves. In His correction of David, what proves God's love the most, is the fact that God had already forgiven David of his sin.

2 Samuel 12:13-14,

"*And David said unto Nathan, I have sinned against the Lord. And Nathan said unto David, The Lord also hath put away thy sin; thou shalt not die. Howbeit, because by this deed thou hast given great occasion to the enemies of the Lord to blaspheme, the child also that is born unto thee shall surely die.*" (KJV)

Oh, how wonderful it is to be loved by God. Even when we do wrong, He loves us the right way. When our sins warrant our death, His grace grants life. What we see next, is that God actually stands in defense of the builder he created; He stands in the line of fire for him. Although the borrower David committed this heinous sin before God, God covers him with grace and state that David's sin brought an occasion for the enemies of God to blaspheme against Him; in other words, David's action caused a reaction not against David, but against God. Since God and not David, because God would not allow it, was blasphemed against, the offspring of sin was required as a sacrifice; it had to die. The sin David loved so much, had to die.

Whether we are talking about the builder or about the person he is anointed to build for; we have all created a mess at some point in our lives, and have loved our messy creation. Many of us have flirted with alcoholism, and conceived the spirit of drunkenness. Some have experimented with sex because of loneliness, and now have become addicted to fornication. Believe it or not, there are some things that we simply should never entertain, but because we've taken our eyes off of God, we become ensnared with the devices of the enemy. Not only do we fall prey to these things, but we love what we do, the mess we make, and the person we become. How many times have we gotten so full of our sinful selves, and declared, 'that's just who I am'? How many alcohol and drug induced parties have we attended because we love to 'let loose, and have a good time'? Well the truth of the matter is that the deposit God has made in the builder requires an interest.

There is a distinguishing mark on the life of the builder that even others can tell the difference, and when that happens; when we are found in love with our mess, God has to intervene because we are causing His enemies to blaspheme against Him. How does that happen? Every time someone points their finger at God's anointed and declare, 'I knew there wasn't anything to them,' God is being blasphemed against; not the person. Each time someone brings a charge against a builder, who happens to be in a borrower's position, they are charging God. But the good news is that He loves us so much, that He takes the heat for us, and in return he requires the complete and total death of our sin.

Instantly, after speaking the word of God to David, God struck the child with an incurable illness; no questions about it, the child was going to die. David loved the child so much that he would not eat or drink while the child was dying. The bible declares that David took off his Kingly robe and laid himself on the floor for seven days. See how hard it is to let go of some things. Stop expecting people in general to change overnight. Some things require a process so be patient, God has already stricken the child; it's dying. In your own life, stop beating yourself up every time you run back to the very thing you should be running from; God has already stricken that child, and it shall surely die. If , perchance you are reading this manuscript on behalf of a borrower, you can tell them that if they would only repent of their ways, and ask God to save their souls, God would hear them and strike the offspring of their sins. No need to wonder when it's going to happen, how it's going to happen, or if it's going to happen. God has too much anointing wrapped up in the builder to allow their character flaws to jeopardize their calling. It will happen. They will put down the cigarettes and the drugs. They will walk away from perversion. They shall have the testimony, 'And it came to pass'!

For seven days, David did not move. Notice how he didn't budge until things were complete? His servants thought he had lost his mind. The King was lying face down in the earth lifeless because his sin, which he loved so much, had to be destroyed. On the seventh day, the child died.

2 Samuel 12:19-20,

"But when David saw that his servants whispered, David perceived that the child was dead: therefore David said unto his servants, Is the child dead? And they said, He is dead. Then David arose from the earth, and washed, and anointed himself, and changed his apparel, and came into the house of the Lord, and worshipped: then he came to his own house; and when he required, they set bread before him, and he did eat." (KJV)

The builder will always find his way back home. After being in the borrower's position, the builder repented of his sins; went into the house of the Lord, and worshipped.

The hardest thing in life to do is the right thing. We error sometimes, but His grace always finds us. Sometimes, the builder can even doubt himself like Thomas, but stop overlooking the fact that he walked with Christ, and then touched him. Once the restored builder in David, reconciled himself with his creator, he did things the right way. Again, he conceived a child with Bathsheba, but this time, God was pleased. In case you didn't know; the child of forgiveness and grace, was named Solomon, who would become the wealthiest, and wisest, builder ever known. Even in a bad situation, God can resurrect a builder whom He loves and honors. Who can call God into question?

You haven't met a prayer warrior better than a builder; just ask Daniel who prayed so much that he got on God's nerves. He prayed until the Lord responded to his plea, and just like the God He is, He dispatched the angel Michael to war on his behalf. Just as an exercise of the anointing that's on your life, if you are in a situation right now that you have been praying for, but nothing has happened yet; open up your mouth and shout, 'God, send Michael.' It's not that He didn't hear you the first time you prayed, but the enemy has held up your deliverance, and therefore; Michael has been dispatched to war against the enemy on your behalf. God, himself, will defend the builder every time; don't believe me; ask Stephen who received stones for his servitude, yet saw God standing up, ready to do battle.

The bible teaches us to know no man after the flesh; that goes for builders as well. Some builders are anointed but have character flaws. Noah was a drunk, Abraham was too old, and even Lazarus was dead at one point, but character flaws aside, God anointed these men to build. These builders, and so many others in the bible, all have something in common; they were called out of their situations, and into the perfect will of God. One thing about being called out is the realization that you were first in something. While many builders are birthed from the womb, many more are either called or converted; case in point; Joshua, whose name only became Joshua after being changed several times. Joshua was the son of Nun.

Now here's a play on words for you. Are you the offspring of parents who were not industry leaders; yet have found yourself in a leading position? Joshua was the son of Nun, or in my case; none, yet he found favor with God and became one of the mightiest biblical leaders of all times. If the builder Joshua were here right now, he would walk around the walls of your Jericho and shout with a loud voice, "Favor, I call upon you to destroy every impenetrable wall of bondage."

Converting a builder requires the direct influence of another builder; like iron sharpening iron. The builder has to be trained in the anointing by which he builds upon. Unfortunately, it requires a process and doesn't happen overnight. Please, don't start judging the man you're with now, because we are not to judge anyone. How can you judge the difference between a borrower and a builder in training?

1 Corinthians 7:14

"For the unbelieving husband is sanctified by the wife, and the unbelieving wife is sanctified by the husband: else were your children unclean; but now are they holy." (KJV)

Your husband, man, significant other, lover, or whatever else you want to call him may be in borrowers' clothes, but can be a builder underneath. The anointing makes the difference, and when the borrower realizes the call on his life, and the anointing of his call, he becomes a builder for the Kingdom of God.

The builder has the power to protect. He is proactive in his ability to secure you from harm. Because of his connection to God, he is pre-warned of incoming attacks from the enemy so when the storm rises, he's already in protection mode. Like Nehemiah, he's highly vigilant with a sword in one hand and building materials in the other. The foundations of your very circumstances could be shaking, but the builder has you anchored in his loving embrace. He is God's ambassador and mouthpiece.

Borrowers impress upon you needless worry. Their intentions are to keep you off target. The more they can get you to focus on things of unimportance, the more they know you will concede. The borrower is a man of redirection. He knows that the complexities of life have inundated you with matters that add stress to your already hectic schedule. You're worried about bills, about your health, and the health of your loved ones. Stress knows no bounds; it adds layers to you as well because now you're stressed about getting the right job, meeting the right people, even finding the right church. You know that you want to worship God, but struggle with religion;

do you go to your grandmother's church, or find your own? Are you even sure that you want to be Pentecostal, or do you feel the call of the Baptist? See how easy it is for the enemy to consume us with clutter; even if the clutter is of good things; in this case, your clutter is religious practice. How do you decide, or do you decide at all? Some feel that all religions are the same anyway.

The builder wants to do for you what Christ did in John 5:6 (KJV), when he simply asked; "Will thou be made whole?" Notice the simplicity and digression from the clutter. We become sidetracked by religion when ministry is staring us right in the face and asking us will we be made whole.

The bible declared in John 5:6, that Christ looked at the man and knew he had been there for a long time. Some of us have suffered some situations for a long time. You've been going through your trials and searching for answers, for a long time. You've already tried pills, suicide, homosexuality, and everything else under the sun, but happiness has still eluded you for a long time. The Christ centered builder already knows that you've suffered long enough and so he's asking you, "Will you be made whole?" He doesn't care about your hang-ups; he doesn't care about how long or short your hair, or your skirt may be; he doesn't even care what church you are a member of; he's simply asking you, will you be made whole?

The religious mind will tell you that the bible teaches us to not be unequally yoked; but have you noticed how they use it to benefit their religion? The wisdom of Christ was on display when he met this man. Notice how Christ never once asked him what religion did he practice, whose church did he go to, or even if he knew who he was? How about that! He didn't even ask the man if he knew that he was the Son of God, or if he believed in him. The only thing on his mind was a soul in need. I mentioned to you how the builder will refocus your mind to what really matters; souls. Be not unequally yoked doesn't mean if you are an Apostolic, you cannot meet a C.O.G.I.C.

builder; it means that builders and borrowers should never be yoked together.

Oh yes, there are some women borrowers as well. How can you spot a woman borrower? She's usually the one who will tear a good man; a builder, into shreds. Her venomous words are like poison to him as they eat away at his masculinity. In words and action; she seduces him, only to reduce him to nothing. The spirit of Delilah is alive in her as she still lulls the builder into relinquishing the anointing as he lays his head in her lap. Jezebel is still in operation today. The generational bitter spirits of Herodias and her daughter Salome, who danced for the head of John on a platter, is still working through some women borrowers. Perhaps at some point and time, you realized that you were a borrower to some degree; all the more reason to want a strong builder who can heal you from the inside out and stop the hemorrhaging.

Some women have become borrowers because of hurt. Some have become borrowers without even realizing how much their past situations have damaged them. If bettered people make better decisions, is it not conceivable that hurt people make decisions from a position of hurt? It is one thing for men to be borrowers, but it is even worse when women are. Why?

This generation has preached that women are equal to their male counterparts; reference the Feminist Movement. No disrespect to any author or celebrity who may write a book, or movie, professing that a woman should act or think, like a man, but the reality is this; that's simply not true. Women are not equal to men in any regards because you're better than we are. Yes, I said it, so there it is. You don't have to think like a man; the truth is, most men don't think; we react.

In my personal opinion, there is a generational falsehood that has been passed down from mother to daughter, and father to son. It states that no one is better than anyone else; we are all the same. I wish that was a reality, but if it is true, then why do we have sporting events to determine the better team? Why is there a difference between good, better, and best? Have you not been taught to always do your best; if so, then what's the difference? Why can you go to any grocery store and purchase a product that is made by different brands, but you've determined that your favorite brand is the best? Yes, there is a realm of better, and the fact remains that women are better than men. You deal with issues better. You internalize situations better. You are naturally better communicators, and that's fine because there are some areas that men are naturally better at. The bottom line is this; what can you do when your better has come under attack? How much more complicated are matters when your better has become your borrower?

Whenever I speak publicly anywhere, I always give honor where it is due. Right after giving honor to God, I am very cognizant to give honor to my wife. The one thing that I do differently, and have taught many other builders, is that you never, ever, reduce her worth by calling her your better half. My wife is the better me! I have a Godly obligation to cover her under the anointing of the builder in me because, in turn, covering my better; produces my best. As a builder, we cannot even begin to operate at our best, until our better is covered, and this is just our reasonable service. There is a reason why the builder must remain prayerful when he covers his wife. He has to know that at some point in their relationship, the enemy will launch an attack against her; trying to destroy the seed.

In planting, we learn through the word of God, all about seed time and harvest, as well as, the type of ground that is conducive for growth. Recently, I planted some apples, tomatoes, onions, and cucumber seeds, in my garden. I wanted to gain a better insight into sowing and reaping, and what I've learned is that all of the seeds planted, required a germination period before sowing them into the ground. In most cases, the seeds that were planted had to have their cover broken first so that new life could begin.

Whether we sow seeds by paying tithes and offering, or supporting another's vision; until the covering of the seed we've sown is broken, no harvest shall grow. The covering of the seed is our attachment to it. Sometimes, we give things or do things with a future attachment associated with it. We sow into ministries, but question where the money is going. We support someone's vision with the expectation that when they get to where they are going, they will in turn, remember us. The ground in these cases, does not make a difference if the seed cover is still intact. The builder knows that the enemy wants us to continue to have an attachment to our seeds. Can't you hear the enemy in your ear convincing you that it's your money; you've worked hard for it? God forbid. If it had not been for the Lord on our side, where would we be? What would we have? Your seed cover must be broken. God would rather you keep your seeds than to sow begrudgingly. When you sow without an attachment, in your season, your harvest will produce residual fruit. He said in His word that He would open up the windows of heaven and pour you out a blessing that you will not have room to receive; so before you begin to sow, allow your seed to mature through the process of breaking the cover over it.

Another seed that the enemy attacks, as mentioned all ready, is the seed of offspring. While the male sperm is considered the seed which fertilizes the egg of the female; on its own, it is worthless. Not only does it require a female counterpart, but once fertilization occurs, it is incubated in the walls of the female's uterus. The replication of life is still a wonder today.

With so many chemical transactions occurring almost instantly, it is hard not to appreciate the great architect who designed the entire system. The sperm meets the egg, causing a cortical reaction which allows only one sperm to fertilize that particular egg; one out of tens of millions. Throughout the differentiation of that egg, DNA is replicated and encoded. If my Bachelors of Science in Biology degree serve me well, then according to the science of Genetics, when the offspring is conceived, it may look, walk, and talk, just like its parents, but be one of a possible 8 million combinations of coding. What is the meaning of all of this?

Scientifically speaking, the enemy hates this entire process because he fears the combined offspring of two God-fearing builders. Of the 40+ million sperm cells that could have penetrated the egg; you made it. Even though the life span of sperm cells, on average, is roughly three days, you made it. Secondly; not only did you make it, but you are uniquely different than your parents, regardless of how much you look just like them. This is why the enemy hates you. You are not here by chance; neither is the builder. But when you and the builder conceive a one of a kind offspring, the enemy fears what that offspring can do because it is now DNA encoded with the best of both of you. You already know you are powerful by yourself, but once the builder joins his anointed DNA with your anointed DNA; the explosive outcome is devastating to the plan of the enemy.

Recall, I mentioned that I would reveal more about the builder/borrower relationship with Leah, Jacob, and Rachel? Here's where the connection continues. While receiving everything he needed as a borrower, Jacob was afforded a builders relationship with Rachel whom he desired. When Rachel mocked Leah, God closed up her womb so that she was barren. After suffering a fruitless marriage and watching her sister conceive now her sixth child, God remember Rachel and He opened up her womb so that they could conceive a child; but not any ordinary child. This child was not only the child of desire; it was a child predestined by God.

Genesis 30:23-24,

"And she conceived, and bare a son; and said, God hath taken away my reproach: And she called his name Joseph; and said, The Lord shall add to me another son." (KJV)

The opening of Rachel's womb is significant in the understanding that even though you can error as a woman, God's will, and His love, takes precedence over your mistakes. Blessing Rachel, who was Jacob's sheer desire, with the ability to reproduce, demonstrates how His plan of provision for your life, will cause the fulfillment of your desires to multiply. It's not until we submit ourselves to the full authority of God, that God will release His purpose for our pain. He's never interested in causing us to suffer, but we have to become fully committed to the call on our lives. The call always produces something greater than who we are.

The builder knows that there is something greater on the inside of you, that you are not even aware of yourself. That's just how in tune with God's plan, this builder is. The child conceived from Rachel's once barren womb; was named Joseph. Joseph had a wearisome life growing up as a young boy, but it was because he was growing up as an anointed builder.

The Builder vs. The Borrower

At an early age, Joseph was favored by his father Jacob, who in turn was favored by God. Being hand-picked by God as a builder, is no easy task; there are some growing pains that the builder has to endure. The storms that the builder must go through aren't designed to destroy, but to reprove and refine the builder for a later and greater purpose. Joseph's testimony is that as a child, he was a dreamer; he had vision. Because he was a dreamer, his brother's hated him. As you can clearly see, there is a recurring theme of hatred being perpetrated against the very elect of God. His brothers collaborated together to take his life, throw him in a pit, and ultimately sell him into slavery for twenty pieces of silver.

The builder is constantly under attack, but never has to look far for their attackers; they're usually close to home. For this reason, the builder must continue to walk softly before God, and be careful that his feet never enter places not meant for his anointing. Joseph went to make peace with his brothers who hated him sorely, but when he entered the city Dothan, he was ambushed and stripped of the coat his father made for him. The enemy is on the lookout; hiding himself in Dothan, waiting for the builder to happen by. Women, pray that the feet of your builder, won't stray into Dothan, no matter how peaceful his message may be.

Joseph, the seventeen year old builder, was sold to Potiphar who was the captain of the guards, and an officer of Egypt's Pharaoh. Even in the builder's Egypt, he is favored by God.

Genesis 39:2,

"And the Lord was with Joseph, and he was a prosperous man; and he was in the house of his master the Egyptian." (KJV)

Only God can bless and prosper you, even in your bondage. To prove that God is an overdoer, not only was Joseph blessed, but even his Egypt prospered from the favor on Joseph's life. Not to be upstaged; the enemy becomes relentless in his attack on the builder. If he can't get you one way, he will go through another. When Josephs' masters' wife had him wrongfully imprisoned, the devil thought he had won, but the glory of God will not be extinguished by the hands, or deeds, of man.

Genesis 39:21-23,

"But the Lord was with Joseph, and shewed him mercy, and gave him favour in the sight of the keeper of the prison. And the keeper of the prison committed to Joseph's hand all the prisoners that were in the prison; and whatsoever they did there, he was the doer of it. The keeper of the prison looked not to any thing that was under his hand; because the Lord was with him, and that which he did, the Lord made it to prosper." (KJV)

Joseph, the builder, would move from the prison to the palace, and all of Egypt was at his fingertips. If, at this point, you are still unable to definitively point out a builder, just look at their life.

If you can see through their history a progression from a prison to a palace, then you have successfully identified the builder. The weight of the anointing on the life of the builder cannot remain in obscurity. When God favors us, His favor of promotion literally catapults us from the bondage we live in, to the Presence He meets us in.

After some time, Joseph's brothers who once sought his demise, had to repent at his feet. Just a quick note in case you were wondering; life, for you, is nowhere near over. Until your foes worship at your feet, life is not over. Some people have entered your life, and have made a mess of it; broke your heart, strung you out, abused you mentally or emotionally, ruined your credit, and took the liberty to do whatever they felt at your expense, but the bible reassures us about the thief:

Proverbs 6:31,

"But if he be found, he shall restore sevenfold; he shall give all the substance of his house." (KJV)

Stop worrying about the house that the borrower caused you to lose; look for the seven that's owed to you. Your car may have been repossessed while you were with the borrower, but look for one seven times better. Isn't it about time that you took God at His word? Mary did just that.

Mary met another builder named Joseph. In case you've heard the story, isn't it ironic that this Joseph just happened to be a builder in the natural as well as in the spiritual? Joseph was a carpenter; he was used to working to the sweat of his brow, but when he fell in love with a woman name Mary, his focused shifted towards building their future together.

Mary experienced some of the harshest ridicule life had to offer. Biblical accounts detail her as an Israelite Jewish woman from Nazareth. Let's first attempt to understand her position. Try explaining the fact that you are a pregnant virgin. Good luck with that one. Who believes you? Can you imagine the whispers; the looks of disgust on the faces of everyone who knew she was Joseph's fiancée? Folks talked about her, hated her, and wanted to stone her to death, believing she was some ordinary harlot; but never understood the extraordinary seed growing within her womb.

I am more than certain, that at times, Joseph was angry, hurt, perplexed, and confused. In some accounts, he was recorded as wanting to divorce her, but instead, he became her builder. The bigger her stomach grew; the more ridicule she faced. The longer the pregnancy dragged on; the more humiliation Joseph had to endure. Her innocence was traded for loathe and distrust. Although something supernatural was happening to her, she had to endure the mockery of a natural world. People just didn't understand. I am sure that Mary didn't understand it herself, but she refused to question God.

Has that ever happened to you? The more you've tried to explain an innocent situation, the more people just didn't understand. The more you've tried to simply fit in with everyone else, the more your stomach stuck out. Before you knew it, you couldn't go anywhere without someone thinking they know everything about you. You felt confused and angry, yet; at the same time, you were happy and excited at the change that was going on inside of you. Your emotions ran wild at the thought of what was happening, but you were forced into a position of shame and depression by everyone around you. Did it seem like everybody had something to say, but no comforting words to offer?

The fact that she was from Nazareth should have been a clear indication that anything was possible. Don't get me wrong; it is much more important to focus on where you are headed than where you are from. What should have came to mind is who you she was connected to. I told you earlier that there was a connection down through the bloodline of generations. No matter how many have tried to sever the connection; God's established bloodline was preserved just for this special moment. Some biblical scholars can trace the connection back to King David, but the truth is that the royal bloodline can be traced all the way back to Adam.

Each generation since Adam, produced a bloodline Prince who was chosen to perform the will of God. Quite notably; each one may have had some form of character flaw, but the perfecting anointing of the builder; made them a Prince in the sight of God. Although each one endured his share of hard trials and tribulations; each one overcame with favor and victory because they were designed by God for their moment.

Builder after builder were established through the bloodline. Some of the builders may have been born in different areas, and into different families, but their connection through the bloodline linked them arm in arm against the enemies of God. Some of the builders were prophets; others were prisoners. Some were warriors, and others were musicians. One even had a problem with speech, and another was the wisest man that ever walked the planet; but they all had one thing in common. They had to prepare the way for the chief builder.

Mary may have been told by an angel about the baby Jesus, but she had no idea of who he really was. Like so many women today; you are in a spiritually pregnant situation, but have no idea of what you are birthing. All of your life lessons have positioned you for this very moment, yet; you still have no idea of what's growing in your spiritual womb. If those people who have hated you, talked about, cursed you out, and did you wrong, only knew how spiritually fertile you really were. When you felt like giving up, it wasn't you; it was just a symptom of your pregnancy. Remember when you grew sick of it all; everybody and everything just made you sick to your stomach; well you were not hallucinating in the least; it was a sure sign of your pregnancy. You've endured so much without cause, that you felt like you were just going to explode. That was another symptom of your pregnancy.

Just like Mary, the enemy fought you with every imaginable device he could get his hands on. People you thought would be in your life forever; turned on you. Friends and loved ones that you have shared so many memorable moments with, now hate you and spread your most intimate secrets every chance they get. You thought you had found true love only to have been used, and abused by another borrower. Well, depending on where you are at the moment, I have some news for you that only you can determine is good or bad; you may want to take a seat for this. You're pregnant!

God has witnessed you being hated and mistreated, and have opened up your womb. He has heard your cry of desperation, and has removed your barrenness; you are now with child. Don't think that the deeds of man have gone unnoticed. God has seen it all, and have responded in kind.

Picture of Nina Tunstalle taken by Jaboy Photography, Institute, WV

You may be thinking that you cannot carry this pregnancy alone, and you are right. That's why God has placed a Joseph; a builder, in your life. Only a builder can cover you while you are spiritually with child.

It takes a bloodline connected builder to rebuild every area that the hatred of man, has torn down. Here comes a Daniel builder to pray you through; a Solomon builder to love you right, or a Joshua builder to secure you from all harm.

The child growing in Mary's womb could only have been secured by a bloodline builder. Joseph almost aborted the mission, but the bloodline arrested his thoughts and pulled him back into builder mode. No matter how difficult times were; no matter how much he had to endure; Joseph could not abandon his bloodline duties. A builder can never abort their mission. This is the life's work of a builder; you have to complete your goal. We may get sidetracked here and there, but we get back on task quickly. Builders may stumble and fall, but they get back into position.

The bloodline connection secures them. The power of the anointing matures them. They are charged with the Godly duty of fulfilling the perfect will of God.

Being that a pregnancy is better assessed by trimesters; I will introduce some of you to the various stages of gestation. Instead of trimesters in the natural, let's consider them "trialsmesters" in the spirit because each round brings new trials and temptations. The different developmental stages of pregnancy depict the active growth and development of the fetus. Physicians are better able to predict such factors as health, and expected due dates, using the trimesters as their main source of gestation analysis.

Logically speaking, Mary could have gotten away during her first trimester because most women don't show during that time. Although the stomach may not protrude, a series of chemical and biological changes are still occurring within the body. Other than the expected symptoms of her pregnancy; outwardly, her appearance during this first trimester could have been normal, but of course, we know that appearances can be misleading.

During your first trialsmester, people will underestimate, and subsequently, undervalue you. No matter how much you have, and are constantly changing on the inside, because they cannot see it outwardly; to them, you're still the same old. They will look right in your face, but not see the change in you. For that reason, this trimester can be the most challenging. It is difficult for you because although you know you've changed, others can't see it. Because they don't see it, they cannot appreciate its value. When you would have normally lashed out, you hold your peace, but people will overlook it. You will have days when you would desire to literally hit the next person that cross you the wrong way, but because there is a Godly fetus growing in your womb, you take the insults, you receive the snide remarks, and you witness the devastation unfolding in your life right before your eyes, but remain unmoved. Even though you are ready to exact revenge, you are going through a series of changes on the inside, which you can't even explain. These changes won't allow the crowning of your anointing to be compromised.

If you are experiencing days when you wake up crying, it's alright; there is a change happening on the inside. You may discover that you have strange and unusual cravings all of a sudden; don't worry, that's part of the change going on inside of you. Without being prompted, you are now craving more of Him, and less of you. If just the very thought of the goodness of Jesus, causes you to break out in fits of worship, don't get alarmed; it's indicative of the cravings associated with the change going on inside of you. Others may not understand what is going on with you, because you can't explain it to them. All you know is that there is a change growing on the inside, and you can't help but to give him glory.

Here's another praise point. Any time there is a change in the natural, an 'exchange' takes place. In other words, in order for a change to occur, something old is exchanged for something new. If I changed my shirt, then I have to take off the old, to put on a new one; even if the new shirt isn't new from the store, it's new on my back. For all of you who are in the middle of change right now, it's time to celebrate because the old, is being exchanged for the new. Your old way of thinking is becoming new. Now imagine just for a moment; there's an exchange occurring inside of you so great, that the entire process gives off glory.

This time frame may appear normal to others, but there's nothing normal about what's growing inside of you. Some women, in the natural, are deemed high risk during this period, and are told by their doctors, to take it easy. I sincerely hope and pray that you can see the symbiotic relationship between the natural and spiritual gestation periods. Sometimes, a high risk pregnancy situation may occur where your body may want to reject the changes going on, and cause a miscarriage of your fetus. Good thing for you that you are under the Doctor's order. He knows that your flesh wants to continue to do some of the things that it has grown accustomed to doing, but He has placed an order of rest on your life.

The second trimester of a woman's pregnancy is filled with extensive biological differentiation. It is during this period when the anatomy of the fetus becomes distinct; no longer does it look like a mass of cells, but body parts are now visible. Along with the extensive differentiation, it becomes harder to conceal the growing fetus. During this period, you may find that your clothes just don't fit the way they used to, and that some of the things you used to consume, now makes you sick. Not only is the fetus going through a rapid succession of chemical and biological changes, but so are you. Outwardly, you're showing that inwardly you're growing. Now, there's no denying that there's something different about you, which opens you up to a new level of scrutiny. No matter how hard you try, you just can't please some people.

During your second trialmester, while the fetus is becoming 'more' developed, your understanding is becoming 'more' clear. Just as the fetus has grown beyond a simple mass of cells, into something more distinguishable, you are now more determined, more prayerful, and more submissive to the will of God. The eyes are developed; so are your spiritual eyes. The legs are formed; so are your spiritual legs. The relationship between you and the growing fetus has intensified so greatly, that you never thought you could love someone, so much. Each night, you may rub your belly in a soothing manner, or find yourself singing praises because you are with child. Your barren season is over.

Others may look at you during this season and wonder who the father may be. Their spiritual eyes cannot see that God has loved you so much; He already placed a ring on it and declared, 'whom I have joined together, let no man put asunder.' Let them shake their heads and talk their talk. Keep your head up Mary, because even the sonogram picture of the fetus, cries Holy! I told you, you didn't even have a clue as to what is growing on the inside of your spiritual womb, but because you're hated.... by now, you should get the picture.

Now we are entering into the third trimester. During this last trimester, the fetus undergoes tremendous growth. What started out as a simple meeting of a seed and an egg has been transformed into new life. Many women find that during this last trimester, their hunger increases; they gain more weight, and their hair grows longer. These are all signs of the last trimester of growth.

If you have experienced any significant growth in your fasting or prayer life; congratulations, you are currently in your final trialmester. When it seems like you cannot get enough of the Word of God; your hunger and thirst for His righteousness has increased, you are in your final trialmester. In the natural, the rise in estrogen causes a pregnant woman's hair to grow. In the spiritual realm, this is no new phenomenon.

Recall I mentioned that I would inform you of the builder Samson's end? Well, the angel of the

Lord told his mother that no razor shall touch Samson's head. As a Nazarene, his hair would continually grow. The source of his strength may have been the bloodline connection of the builder, but the telltale sign of it, was his hair. Just as with the builder Samson, as your hair grows, so does your strength. While many people are still under the assumption that his death was the end of him; I beg to differ. Down through the bloodline of the builder Samson; the connection continued to the baby Christ. The chief builder Christ, who also grew up in Nazareth, is the end of Samson, and all other builders. This is why the enemy fights you so hard in the beginning; because he knows that your end is Christ. Just imagine for a moment, what you have growing on the inside of you? This is the reason why God has established a builder, just for you. What you are pregnant with; only a builder can protect.

If Mary only knew what was growing within her. Just like Mary, some of you will give birth to your own miracle. Some women will birth out their own healing. The enemy could only wish that he had destroyed your pregnancy in the beginning, because you are about to deliver the destroyer of his kingdom. Many of you have been troubled and perplexed, but you are pregnant with your own peacemaker. At the appointed time, the good Doctor will tell you that now, is the time to push.

During the delivery phase, sometimes, the woman wants to push through a contraction, but is told that the time has not arrived yet; either you're not fully dilated, or the baby is in the wrong position. Being fully dilated helps you during the delivery process because it ensures that your body has fully positioned itself. When the baby is in the wrong position, it could mean the life of your offspring. Eating from everyone's table in the spiritual; is the wrong position for your offspring. It dies. Casting your pearls before swine, is the wrong position for your offspring. It dies.

Some of your contractions are excruciating; I told you in the beginning that you already endure some things that man cannot. For the health and well-being of you and your offspring, the doctor will not allow you to push before the baby is in the birthing position.

Picture of baby Mila taken by Kelli Carrico Photography. Beckley WV

The Builder vs. The Borrower

The builder is the one who is always there with you; from the first day of your pregnancy, through delivery. Do you see the resemblance between him and his creator who said in Matthew 28:20,

"...lo, I am with you alway, even unto the end of the world." (KJV)

This is not a manuscript of suggestions. This is reality; and in your reality, you can bear witness that if it had not been for the Lord on your side, there would have been an increase in the homicide statistics. The number of suicides would have escalated sharply. If God had not kept your mind, the mental institutions would have ran over. That's how much He loves you despite of your character flaws. He has assigned a builder to walk with you, every mile of the way. Let the naysayers talk as they will, Tamar. Despite what they may think, you've proven that you are more righteous than Judah.

For those women whose faith has died because of the borrower, it's not too late. He may have caused your prayer life to cease to exist, but there's still a Peter who can speak life into your dead places again; just ask the disciple Tabitha. In the book of Acts, she was described as being a woman of good deeds; yet, she died. Some of you have had good intentions that have died. You may have had a good fasting life, but since your entanglement with the borrower, it has died within you. Your dreams, your goals, your future plans of success; all have died within you. Remember when you were going to start that business; you ran well, but who hindered you? When you were going to go back to school, who talked you out of it? All of your good works; pleasant attitude; even your very demeanor, have all been affected by the borrower, and only the builder Peter, can come along and revive where you have lost life. Your family and friends may have good intentions, but they don't understand. All they can do is what Tabitha friends did; they watched and wept. Even when they brought the builder Peter into the upper chamber where her lifeless body was laid; they watched and wept. They showed Peter the coats and garments that she made while she was yet alive.

Whether you want to believe it or not, you have some dead areas within you now, but your acquaintances can only watch and weep. Every now and again, they may go as far as to remind you of the good things that you used to do. Remember when you did this? Do you remember when we had that? They don't understand that they're only presenting your good works; the coats and garments that you've made while you were still living. There are two very important factors that need to be considered; either they don't understand who you are, or won't accept what this builder is capable of.

Acts 9:39-40,

"*Then Peter arose and went with them. When he was come, they brought him into the upper chamber: and all the widows stood by him weeping, and shewing the coats and garments which Dorcas made, while she was with them. But Peter put them all forth, and kneeled down, and prayed; and turning him to the body said, Tabitha (interpreted to mean Dorcas), arise. And she opened her eyes: and when she saw Peter, she sat up."* (KJV)

You don't have to believe or receive, but blessed are those who do because there is a builder named Peter who is standing by to declare that your hopes, and ambitions, will not die. The builder never asked what her goals in life were, he simply said get up, and everything dead within Tabitha had to awaken. The builder that is assigned to you will immediately speak to those dead areas in your life and declare they shall live. You will open that business. You might as well start looking at colleges because you will go back to school.

After the builder Peter presented her alive again to her family and friends, many then, believed in God; Acts 9:41-42 (KJV). In other words, when your builder revives what's dead inside of you, many will follow Jesus. So, it's not that you haven't been doing your best to witness to your friends; your builder just hasn't spoken life into your dead areas yet. You may have preached and taught a good word but still have wondered why people around you just haven't gotten it; your Peter hasn't revived those dead areas yet. When your builder revives those dead or dry areas in your life; without having to utter a single word, people will just see you and know that God is real. There will be such an anointing over your life that folks who once hated you, will worship at your feet. You think you have a prayer life now; just wait until the builder speaks life to it. You think you are on the road to success now; just wait until your Peter prophesy life to it and tell it to arise.

Do you know who is sitting upon your well asking you for drink? Don't let the shame of your past relationships and decisions, make you alienate yourself from everyone else. The Samaritan woman went to the well alone, because she had a troubled past. Her decision-making process wasn't the best by far. Perhaps, there was some devastating circumstance in her childhood that altered her ability to choose the right husband.

Some of the hardships of your past have driven your decision-making process in the wrong direction at some point too; it has happened to all of us. The fact that she had married several times before, caused her to withdraw from everyone around her because of shame. So, she went to draw water from the well alone; thinking she could hide herself, but while she was there, she had an unusual encounter with the Chief Builder.

Have you ever had a totally unexpected encounter with God? Though it is not written in the scriptures, I can assume with great confidence that she chose men after men; trying to find something that only the builder could have fulfilled. How do I know that for sure? While she was at the well, she did two things that clued me in. The first thing that she did, demonstrated her low self-esteem when she asked him, 'why would you ask me, a Samaritan woman, to give you drink?'

John 4:9,

"Then saith the woman of Samaria unto him, How is it that thou, being a Jew, askest drink of me, which am a woman of Samaria? for the Jews have no dealings with the Samaritans." (KJV)

One of the greatest hindrances in ministry is our own perception of us. We see ourselves through the eyes of our mistakes, and become crippled by our own discernment. Some of us don't have to wait for others to render us helpless because we surrender our own authority to our past mistakes. We believe in our words that God is a forgiver of our transgressions, but in our hearts, we think we've gone just a little too far this last time; we fell just a little too low this last time. We then judge ourselves by our faults instead of our favor with God. The next thing we know, all of our past choices becomes the basis of our self-esteem. There are so many of us, who are suffering from low self-esteem, and are not even aware of it. This

Samaritan woman must have had some experiences in her past that drove her to her current position.

The next thing that leaped out at me was the fact that she tried to hide the fact that she was already married. This told me that she was still searching for something that only a builder could provide.

John 4:17-18,

"The woman answered and said, I have no husband. Jesus said unto her, Thou hast well said, I have no husband: For thou hast had five husbands; and he whom thou now hast is not thy husband: in that saidst thou truly." (KJV)

Not only did the Chief Builder know that she was hiding, he knew what she was hiding and how it affected her perception. When you are in the presence of the builder, you no longer have to hide who you are, what you did, or how you feel; he already knows, and it's his assignment to rebuild those damaged areas.

Now, let's put some things in perspective. Is there anything that this builder cannot do? The answer is yes. The builder cannot do more than what you are willing to allow him to do on your behalf. He is a true gentleman. He can handle anything; but when you begin to limit his involvement, he doesn't force himself to resolve them. Just as with the Holy Ghost, you have to allow the builder the right of way. Stop treating him like the borrower before him; he's not; nor is he the father who left you when you were young.

It's not a hard thing to love you. The builder desires to make you whole again, but he wants to do it according to the will of God for your lives together. He's a provider; a nurturer; and a mender. He will never lift a finger against you because he loves the ground you stand upon. He is charged with an assignment from God to love you to your soul. Men are either one or the other; builder or borrower. There is no in-between. Those of us anointed to build; build.

You have a voice and a choice to make. Your thoughts and dreams do matter, and it's only the builder who can ensure, through the grace of God, that it comes to pass. There's nothing more securing than being in the arms of the man who's safely in the arms of God.

There's an expression that I am more than certain, you've heard many times before; 'never live above your means'. That term has been passed down through the ages as some form of wisdom, and in our limited thinking capacity, it makes perfect sense. Well, I challenge that notion by the authority of God. This notion is usually based on income, as in money. Favor cannot be reduced to simple dollars and cents. Therefore; when we are in the perfect will of Christ, why do we categorize ourselves by the earthly standards of means? Means; as in what sustains us? Well, when we are a new creation in Christ, does He not sustain us? Is He not the provider, or the lover of our souls, that He said He would be?

If Christ is the head of our lives, as a builder, we are kept under His shadow. He feeds us; hides us, and protects us from all harm. Therefore; He is the only means by which we exist, and if that is the case, then how can we live above Him? In actuality, sadly enough, many of us live too far beneath our means; or our God. We aspire to just live in His submissive will, as if His perfect will is just too far out of our reach. Oh yes, God has a submissive will where we are allowed limited access, but His perfect will is where He desires us to be. No, this is not a prosperity pitch; it's a reality check.

Just look around yourself. Take a good look at where you are, where you live, and how you are living. Take an honest assessment. Are you where you have always imagined yourself to be? Are you in the house of your dreams, or do you desire more? Do you drive your dream car, or have you settled for making the costly repairs needed to keep what you have, running? While we have found grace, and are being sustained where we are, if it's not where we desire to be, then we are in the submissive will of God.

Psalms 84:11,

"For the Lord God is a sun and shield: the Lord will give grace and glory: no good thing will he withhold from them that walk uprightly" (KJV)

If you are not where you desire to be, please don't confuse where you are, as not walking uprightly. That's my point exactly. You can be doing everything you know that is right according to the word of God, and still find yourself not where you want to be in life. If this is the scenario you have found yourself in, then you must ask yourself whether or not you have truly applied the principles of God. For one, with a sincere heart; have you truly asked so that if can be given to you, because He stated in His word, that there is a blessing so great, you won't have room to receive it.

The next point I want to ask you is about your vision. Do you honestly have one? Here's a measuring point for vision; if your vision is no larger than yourself, then it's not a vision; that's an illusion. Anyone with a vision understands that the vision is so large, that it has to be written down so that others can see it and run; you can reference Habukkah 2:2. A vision is greater than who you are, and where you currently are. Think about it in the natural. Let's suppose that you desire to start a business but you don't have all the money you need for startup. Here again, is where we as believers use earthly standards to justify our calling in God. Like some of us, we stop right here at this point. This is what I mean by submissive will. We are doing what He commands but only believing Him to provide for us right here, and why? Why do we reduce the favor of God on our lives under the auspices of a very limited monetary system; especially when the dollar rate fluctuates daily? We used to sing. 'On Christ the solid rock I stand. All other ground is sinking sand'.

Then, there are those who press beyond this initial point and find ways around not having the money to start their vision, to become widely successful. That's indicative of his perfect will. If He gave you the vision, He's God enough to provide provision. Living in His perfect will, means that you have to learn to take the limits off of God.

God's perfect will for us is only found through total surrender. There's no amount of money you can tithe, or prayer you can pray; He desires total access to your life. The hardest thing for many of us to do is to arrest ourselves, and totally surrender all to the will of God. We are too plagued with having to 'live' in the real world, when we read in His word, how He has repeatedly made provisions for those whom He loved. That seriously begs the question; how much do we really trust God? Can we really trust someone, or something, that we cannot see? Many of us claim that we do, but in actions; we don't. We profess week after week, how much we love Him in our worship services, but seem to fall short of displaying it during the week.

When we fully surrender to God; I mean heart, mind, and soul, we are found in His perfect will for our lives. While I am no preacher of prosperity; there is prosperity in the perfect will of God; not just prosperity in the natural sense, which many of us can only fathom, but in the spirit.

3 John 1:2-4,

"Beloved, I wish above all things that thou mayest prosper and be in health, even as thy soul prospereth. For I rejoiced greatly, when the brethren came and testified of the truth that is in thee, even as thou walkest in the truth. I have no greater joy than to hear that my children walk in truth." (KJV)

You don't have to take my word for it; like you, I am inclined to let every man be a liar, and God be the truth. Jesus, the Chief Builder, openly displayed who He was, and what He was sent to do. Being the only Son of God, and Chief Builder, He healed the sick, gave sight to the blind, fed multitudes just by giving thanks, and performed many more miracles, but found himself, as most builders, in quite an unusual situation. In the third book of John, He admits that He wish you would prosper.

Think about this; why would you have to wish for something you can simply obtain? Does it make sense to wish for a steak dinner, when you can hop in the car and head out to your favorite steak restaurant? My point is this; wishes are made for things that are seemingly out of our reach; it's just a bit beyond our abilities to perform. As much as I would love to be able to cure cancer, I could only wish that cancer was completely eradicated, because that's just beyond my ability to perform. Why then, does the Son of God; the same Son of the same God who has everything, and can do anything, only wish that you would prosper? He does so because the choice to willingly submit ourselves to Him lies with us; not even the Chief Builder can force himself on you. The dividing line is our ability to choose. To make it as plain as possible, He is telling us that He has one thing in store for us, or we can have things our way; either way He loves us – He proved that by dying for our sins, but one road leads to His perfect will over our lives and the other road leads to what He allows for us.

The Chief Builder is found in the hearts and minds of every builder created. He is the center of the builder and His presence, can be felt through him. Having the builder in your life makes believing in the Chief Builder, easier. It's as if; when you touch the face of the builder in your life, you are touching the very face of God, and for that cause alone, you find yourself not wanting to do anything to damage his love for you. Isn't it a wonderful feeling to be in love? When you cry, the builder cries. When you laugh; the builder laughs with you. When you are afraid, the builder covers you in his arms. He talks to you; comforts and listens to you. The builder asks you, 'how was your day', and if it was bad, he then asks, 'what can I do to make it better?' No doubt he loves you; he not only says it, but openly proves it each and every chance he gets. His mission from God is to love you like the Chief Builder loves the church. You are indeed his bride. It's ok to give your heart to the builder; things will work this time. It's alright to fall in love again, as long as it's with the builder for your life; you won't be able to help it anyway because his love, is the love of God, and anytime we find ourselves in the presence of God, we tend to discover that we have a bad case of the, 'I just can't help myself.'

While the builder has made room for you, you have to make room for him; in fact, it begins with you. You have to be in a position of expectancy before the builder arrives. No, I am not saying that you have to go find him; that's where many women have erred. They have sought after whom they believed were the one for them, but have only found borrowers.

Just a quick question out of curiosity. I am a huge proponent of the idea that once you know how a person acts; what they do should not affect you. So, if you knew that I was an alcoholic, then why would my drinking affect you? Wouldn't you come to expect me to drink? Now, my question is this; if you know that you went about the relationship you were in, or are currently in, the wrong way, then why wouldn't you expect him to be a borrower? What's even more amazing is that we get bent out of shape, want to fight and argue; cry and get depressed, over a borrower. No matter how much you try; you cannot change a borrower into a builder; only God can do that, and if you have found yourself in a Godless relationship, then why would you expect more?

I had the privilege to speak with a young woman some time ago, regarding her relationship. My question to her was simple, 'do you think you deserve the best?' As simple a question this may be, you should really take an introspective look into yourself before answering because some women don't think so. Some women think that they deserve whatever they get in life, as if it were some punishment for something they did that was so wrong. God doesn't want to punish you; He wants to love you like you've never been loved before. He doesn't care about what you did, how you did it, or who you did it to; He just wants you so much, that He hand-carved a replica of himself in the form of a builder, just for you.

Do you think you deserve the very best? If your answer to this question is yes, then why would you settle for someone who isn't? The borrower may be fun, but he's not the best that God has for you. Your kids may even like your borrower friend, but they will love your builder. You do not have to settle anymore. I don't care if the builder that's designed for you is currently working at a fast food restaurant; he's still your builder. No, that doesn't mean that you will have to give up your house, and live off of his income. The first thing you should do, is not be so judgmental over those things you don't know for sure. Just because he's working in a fast food restaurant, doesn't mean he's not the owner of it, or a chain of them, but just in case he is only an employee, understand that his assignment from God begins and ends with you. Perhaps, by chance, he was sent there by God, and told to wait until you got yourself together, and when the two of you were ready, the Chief Builder will begin to add the increase. Yes; by default, some of you have builders stuck in a holding pattern because you're not ready to receive them. So how do you ready yourself?

There's a worship song we used to sing in church that said, 'So, forget about yourself, concentrate on Him, and worship Him.' You have to first forget those things which are behind you.

Philippians 3:13-14,

"Brethren, I count not myself to have apprehended: but this one thing I do, forgetting those things which are behind, and reaching forth unto those things which are before, I press toward the mark for the prize of the high calling of God in Christ Jesus" (KJV)

As sure as you have lived, there are some things in your past that seemingly find their way to your present. You have to take the advice of the builder Paul, the Chief Apostle, and forget about everything yesterday. Sure, you made mistakes; we all have, but that's so yesterday and it has no place in your future. How long are you going to let one bad choice from long ago, define who you are today?

Once you make the clear choice of letting go of your past, then you are on the path towards being made whole. The next thing you should do is get rid of everything that reminds you of your borrower. Return his rings, his jewelry, his clothing; even his socks and shoes. Get rid of anything that resembles everything you've ever experienced with the borrower. This will keep you from wanting to remember. Sometimes, we can't trust our own memories. When we get lonely enough, we begin to reminisce about some things we shouldn't want to recall. The feeling of nostalgia creeps in every time we see something that belongs to the borrower. The main reason why you can't trust your memory sometimes is because; in our minds, we remember things as we wish they were; not as they actually happened. You could try to remember all the good times you had with the borrower, but in reality, do you remember the nights you spent bandaging your wounds because he beat you unconscious? You can try to make yourself believe that every word out of the borrower's mouth said I love you, but in reality he was too busy calling you out of your name; do you remember that?

It's time to stop holding on to those things that remind you of him; let it go. The truth is this; if you don't let the memory of the borrower go, then you are prone to try and find another borrower to replace him. Do you know any of your sisters who have ended up with the same type of man over and over again? It's because they've never let go of the first borrower. Forget about the things from your past, and press forward.

By now, some of you may be feeling that unnerving sensation of not knowing what to do next. You're not sure of relationships, friendships, kinships, or even battleships at this point. You may have decided to change some things in your life, but now, have no clue as to what you are going to do next. Believe it or not; now you are exactly where you are supposed to be; totally dependent on God. If you make all the plans for your life, then why would you need God? His plan; supersedes our agendas. You are now refocusing, and are able to see things differently.

Another habit that must be broken is the habit of nomenclature. From biblical times through today, your name affiliates you with family, or status. It could get you in places or bar you from places all together. Even the bible speaks of having a good name.

Proverbs 22:1,

"*A good name is rather to be chosen than great riches, and loving favour rather than silver and gold.*" (KJV)

Names are more or less, indicators of time nowadays. The names that we were given, and some of us even earned in our childhood, no longer apply to who we are today. Stop feeling as if you have to answer to a name from your past; you are no longer your mistake. So what if some don't see the change in you; does that refute the evidence of change? I understand that some things seem so harmless and innocent, but when you begin to grow in maturity with God, childish things must cease. You're no longer required to answer to 'lil tay tay' or even, 'ain't you the girl that used to....'

Once you have an encounter with God, you go through a name changing ceremony. He changes your name for His glory. Not only does He give you a new name, as He repeatedly did in the bible, He then writes that name down in the Lamb's Book of Life.

So, you can tell sickness; that's no longer your name. Broken hearted, angry, depressed; these are no longer your name. You've met God face to face, and like Moses, you don't even look the same. Your hair has changed and your countenance has changed, so why would you settle to still be called by bitterness, envious, or easy? You are not the sum total of your mistakes. You are the evidence of the only thing that can still wash away all of our sins. In preparation for your builder, allow the cleansing power of the blood of Jesus, to wash away every memory, every resemblance, every detail of your past, every trace of hurt; everything that your name once depicted you to be.

2 Corinthians 5:17,

"Therefore if any man be in Christ, he is a new creature: old things are passed away; behold, all things are become new." (KJV)

Start forgiving people in your life, and stop holding on to the fact that they've wronged you. Man will fail every time, yet; God forgives us. For many women, this area has become an issue. Forgiving people does not mean the same as, 'I forgive you, but I just don't want to be bothered.' Who are you? Suppose God said the same to us; and He's the only one that has the right to do so. Suppose He said, 'I forgive you, but I don't want to be bothered with you.' God not only forgives us, but He forgets our debts.

Hebrews 8:12,

"For I will be merciful to their unrighteousness, and their sins and their iniquities will I remember no more." (KJV)

If God can truly forgive us of our sins, then we should be able to truly forgive others of their transgressions against us. We're not perfect people; we're a people worth perfecting.

While you are starting a habit of forgiving people; begin by forgiving yourself. Stop thinking it's your fault. Yes, your life is worth living. It's not the end of the world, but this is the end of your loneliness. Give yourself another chance; you are worthy. You are royalty. There is someone; a builder, fighting his way into your life. You will love again. You don't have to beat yourself up anymore because of what happened last night. Every morning brings us a brand new mercy. It's time for you to start living in the perfect will of God; that's where your blessings lie. Despite what anyone may think, the word of God has already declared that you are the head and not the tail; the lender and not the borrower. Adorn yourself in His righteousness and wait for your change to come.

You may be thinking that it's easier said than done, but I assure you, that you can do it. You can make it this time. Now, you are equipped with the knowledge to withstand the wilds of the adversary. Prosperity is within your bosom, as you are clothed in victory. You have the power to reverse the order of your life. You're strong in the Lord, and He's proud of you.

Until your handmade builder arrives on your doorstep, you are still covered under the anointing of the Chief Builder who is the architect of your soul. No more crying now; you've made it. No more sickness can hold you now; you are more than a conqueror. The borrower can't take anything else from you no more. The anointing of this builder, rebukes him. You shall have life. You will nurse your heart's desire.

If you are reading this book for the first time and do not have a relationship with the Chief Builder, then let me introduce you to Mary's baby. He is Jehovah Jireh. He is the wheel in the middle of the wheel. He's the chief cornerstone; the bright and morning star. He's the reason why Lazarus got up, and Bartimaeus could see. He is our redeemer and the lover of our souls. If I spent the rest of my days here on earth describing who He is, I would have to borrow a few lifetimes just to scratch the surface. He's the designer of your builder; He knows just what you need.

Until that glorious time of introduction comes, encourage yourself. After all the things you've been through, you deserve a compliment. That's just what your builder is; a compliment. He is that final piece in your puzzle that makes the whole picture make sense. If you know you have a borrower in your heart, or in your home right now, tell him his borrowing days are over. You don't have to allow him access to your possessions any longer. You have the authority now; you've always had it, you just didn't operate in it.

Now, is the season of your greatest release and subsequent increase! How do I know this to be true? I was a borrower for many years because I didn't understand the anointing on my life. I borrowed from women, from churches, and everything in between; worst of all; I didn't even know I was a borrower.

I grew up in church but because I was a borrower, I didn't let the church grow up in me. I was too wounded in my childhood to understand what was genuine and pure. As far as I could tell, everyone had an agenda, and I was tired of receiving the short end of the stick.

As a borrower, you hurt other people, whether intentionally or not. I spent years in depression as a borrower. I thought as a borrower; lived like a borrower, and could only produce the little that a borrower could produce. My life was going nowhere, and I was at the wheel; driving it there fast.

Sure, I knew all about church, I was a minister of music. I was afforded the opportunity through my gift of music, to play before great men. I've played music before African Kings and Queens, as well as, at a White House event. My extensive musical resume displays that I've played all over this great country, but the fact still remained, that I was just a music playing borrower – I didn't understand the anointing over my life. At one devastating point; I didn't even want to accept it. I didn't want anything to do with church, with music, with ministry, or with God. As harsh as this testimony may seem, I must share this in hopes that others can identify themselves as borrowers, and begin to allow God to convert them into builders.

I had money; I drove fancy cars, and at one point; could have had whatever I wanted in life – life was good, but I was still a borrower. I didn't even understand that during those times, it was God who had provided for me. In my cockiness, it was all me. I walked out of church after experiencing a devastating hurt, and declared that there is no God. If there was a God, then why would he allow me to go through what I had to experience? Where was He when I needed him to stand in my defense?

I moved on with my life, but called myself moving on without God. As mentioned in this book, the anointing over your life is undeniable. I tried to forget all about God, but I am so glad that He never forgot about me.

One day, I was in a dance club in my hometown of Washington DC, and I thought I was having a good time. I had my boys with me; some money in my pocket, a drink in one hand, and a girl on the dance floor; surely this was going to be a night for the books. The DJ started playing a fan favorite, old school song, and we started dancing. Sounds like a good time, right?

While the music was still playing, the girl, whom I didn't know at all, turned around, looked me in my eyes and said, 'what are you doing here? You don't belong here.' Then she turned and walked away. Instantly, I was taken back. In my mind, she didn't know me. How dare she say where I belong; who did she think she was? It wasn't until later on that evening that it hit me like a ton of bricks. What was I doing to myself? How in the world could I try to forget God?

Me, being the borrower I was, I shook that one random experience off and tried to put it behind me. I didn't grow up rebellious at all; in fact, I was a great kid; straight A's in school, no trouble at home, and have never used any drugs in my life. On the surface, I was ideal, but I was broken by the memory of being molested between the ages of 5-10 years old. Abuse is abuse in any form; and when I was married to my first wife, I was physically abused in that relationship as well, and that was through the church. How could the same God that loved me so much, punish me so cruelly as to revive my brokenness; so I rebelled for the first time in my life.

Please don't misunderstand; I am not conjuring an excuse for being a borrower, but I want to break the bondage of that borrowing spirit through this testimony. A week had passed since that nightclub episode; and don't worry, I never went back there again. I was still reeling from that episode, when I had to travel to Baltimore for an evaluation. I walked into a medical facility in the downtown area of Baltimore, in jeans, a pullover shirt, sneakers and a baseball cap. As soon as I entered the building, someone whose loved one was clinging to life, was roaming the hallway, and as I passed by them, they turned around and grabbed me by the arm. Immediately, I turned around and looked at them, thinking that they were crazy, but then they opened their mouth with tears in their eyes and said, 'excuse me sir, are you the minister I've been waiting for?' I wanted to push them off of me, but my heart was pricked, and I answered, 'yes'.

Since that day, I have repented for doubting the will of God in my life. He has proven to me over and over again, that I am His, and He is mine. I know that He loves me, because He's keeping me alive. When I finally submitted myself to his will, he crowned me a builder and gave me an assignment to build.

I have had some good days and some not so good days since being a builder, but through it all, He has proven himself to be God in my life. I didn't make every right decision, and I want the builders out there to know that every choice you make may not be right, but because we have access to His Grace, we are allowed to get back up and build again. I've suffered some heavy losses since being a builder, but I'm still building. Some of the setbacks I've experienced were because of the enemy's setups, but I am still building.

If God can do it for me, He can do if for the builder assigned to your life. Keep believing God and holding on to His words; not mine. In due season, your builder will come. Keep the faith. Trials don't last always and neither will this storm. Hold your head up, no matter how much it hurts. No matter how much you have to cry your way through it at night; endure hardships as a good soldier. As my grandmother would say, 'Payday', or in this case, your builder, is coming after a while. God bless you!

~ Pastor Gregory W. Covington II ~

ABOUT THE AUTHOR

Photo of Gregory W. Covington II by Ormando International, Raleigh, NC

Mr. Gregory W. Covington II believes that the crucibles of life, brings out the absolute best in us. A native of the District of Columbia; Mr. Covington continues to lead and mentor countless individuals in the areas of business, relationships, spirituality, and life. Using his arsenal of education and experience, Mr. Covington is a professional author, speaker, musician, and so much more.

Born in October 1974, to parents Alice and Gregory Sr., Mr. Covington knows the importance of having a determined spirit. As a child, 'Greg' as he often refers to himself, exhibited the charismatic leadership style that he is known for today. Although there were years of his childhood filled with abuse, Greg overcame those obstacles and used those devices of destruction as stepping stones to success. In fact, one of the most humbling experiences Mr. Covington can recall is being ordained as a Pastor in 2005.

Today, Mr. Covington has earned a Bachelor's of Science degree in Biology from the University of Charleston, a Master's of Science degree in Strategic Leadership from Mountain State University, a Master's of Science in Accounting from Walden University, and is currently completing his Doctorate of Business Administration with a specialization in

Finance. He plans to take the CPA exam in the Spring of 2014. Although his educational background may seem quite an accomplishment to many, Mr. Covington is most proud of the fact that he was the first in his generation to simply graduate high school; a proven giant slayer. He continues to be an inspiration as he travels the country giving lectures on issues ranging from Domestic Violence, to Strategic Leadership.

One of the most prolific speakers of today, Mr. Covington has called the suburbs of Durham, NC, home. He can be seen fishing on his off days, or spending quality time with his wonderful wife and kids. Together, he and his wife, have raised not only their own children, but have been surrogate parents to so many others who were abused, troubled, or otherwise hurting. An exemplary pastor with a passion for people, Mr. Covington proves that hard work and determination are the main ingredients to success. When asked what's next, Mr. Covington jokingly replied, "What's next? I haven't done anything yet; I'm just getting warmed up."

For more information on upcoming book releases, you can follow Mr. Covington on Twitter @drgwayne2, or "Like" his Facebook page, Author G.W. Covington II

For booking information, please contact:

Corretta

(301)803-9409

Corretta@TheAListInc.com

www.TheAListInc.com

The A List, Inc.

6051 Business Center Court

Suite 4324

San Diego, California 92154

Strategic Business Management and Consulting

www.ingramcontent.com/pod-product-compliance
Lightning Source LLC
Chambersburg PA
CBHW031513040426
42445CB00009B/203